Reading Shakespeare

Michael Alexander

Emeritus Professor of English Literature
University of St Andrews

First published 2013 by
PALGRAVE MACMILLAN

Palgrave Macmillan in the UK is an imprint of Macmillan Publishers Limited, registered in England, company number 785998, of Houndmills, Basingstoke, Hampshire RG21 6XS.

Palgrave Macmillan in the US is a division of St Martin's Press LLC, 175 Fifth Avenue, New York, NY 10010.

Palgrave Macmillan is the global academic imprint of the above companies and has companies and representatives throughout the world.

Palgrave® and Macmillan® are registered trademarks in the United States, the United Kingdom, Europe and other countries.

ISBN 978–0–230–23012–5   hardback
ISBN 978–0–230–23013–2   paperback

This book is printed on paper suitable for recycling and made from fully managed and sustained forest sources. Logging, pulping and manufacturing processes are expected to conform to the environmental regulations of the country of origin.

A catalogue record for this book is available from the British Library.

Library of Congress Cataloging-in-Publication Data
Alexander, Michael, 1941–
Reading Shakespeare / Michael Alexander.
p. cm.
ISBN 978–0–230–23013–2 (pbk.)
1. Shakespeare, William, 1564–1616—Examinations—Study guides.
2. Shakespeare, William, 1564–1616—Criticism and interpretation.
I. Title.
PR2987.A47 2012
822.3′3—dc23   2012032196

10 9 8 7 6 5 4 3 2 1
22 21 20 19 18 17 16 15 14 13

Printed and bound in China

Benedictus benedicat

Contents

List of Illustrations and Tables

Illustrations

Tables

Preface

This is a book on reading Shakespeare, on Shakespeare as read, on Shakespeare through reading. For students, as for many others, this is how Shakespeare first appears, as words on a page; later, as performance on a stage. Reading the printed words involves imagining an action – imagining it as fully as possible, imagining the words as spoken.

Reading Shakespeare introduces 20 of Shakespeare's 39 plays, and his Sonnets, prefaced by a sketch of his life and of the theatre of his day. It is not written for the specialist, and its aim is to be helpful rather than novel. It brings in contexts of an historical, cultural and literary kind, but keeps its eye on what immediately arises from the reading of the text of a play or a poem. Plays are especially open to variety in interpretation. There is no exclusively right reading of a play, least of all of a play by Shakespeare, though there are mistaken readings.

The focus of this book, as its title suggests, is on the experience of reading the plays. William Shakespeare first put himself before the public by publishing two long narrative poems and putting his name to them. The poems proved popular and were often reprinted. By 1594 he had a name as a poet. His new plays now went into print: 18 of his plays were printed in his lifetime, half of these being reprinted. In all, at least 39 editions of single plays by Shakespeare appeared before his death in 1616. In the collected edition of his drama, the famous First Folio of 1623, the 18 already published plays were joined by 18 not previously published.

Readers of Shakespeare's plays assume that he wrote them to be read as well as performed. Performance has been a focus of recent Shakespeare scholarship, seeing him rather as a scriptwriter for the theatre of the Early Modern period than as a poetic dramatist of the Renaissance – different descriptions of the same animal. The texts of his plays have also been approached less as the product of a writer, more as a by-product of company performance. These emphases correct a purely literary approach. Yet many of

Shakespeare's plays were published in the 1590s, so he wrote for readers as well as for performance. Some of these plays are literary in another way, their success depending upon the recognition of stylistic parody, as in scenes of *Love's Labour's Lost*, *A Midsummer Night's Dream* and *Henry IV*. A fully literary status for Shakespeare's plays was asserted in the Folio of 1623. Ben Jonson, in his prefatory verses, 'To the memory of my beloved, the Author, Master William Shakespeare', placed him above all other European dramatists, classical or contemporary, claiming that 'He was not of an age, but for all time.'[1] After four centuries, this claim does not seem as presumptuous as it must have sounded in 1623.

Reading and performance are reciprocal parts of the one process, each feeding and needing the other. This introduction to Shakespeare treats his play-texts as dramatic literature for imaginative reading. A play's text is the formula for its physical enactment, a formula enabling theatrical revival; but it is also more. A sense of what an emphasis on performance can leave out may be what led a Swiss scholar, Lukas Erne, to conceive his *Shakespeare as Literary Dramatist*, published in 2003.[2] The need for a book with such a title might once have seemed surprising, but the book is persuasive in documenting the evidence that Shakespeare wanted his plays to be read as well as seen, arguing also that he produced long versions of *Hamlet* and *King Lear* – too long to be acted. Erne also shows that by 1598 Shakespeare's plays were praised as literature and anthologised as such: extracts from them appeared in *England's Parnassus*, 1600, an anthology of non-dramatic verse, and another similar anthology. Jonson's claim that we should see the drama of Shakespeare as the supreme classic of European literature was accepted by John Dryden, who died in 1700, and assumed by Alexander Pope, who edited all the plays in 1723. Greek tragedy was part of Greek literature and Shakespeare's plays were part of English literature. So much was taken for granted by John Keats when in 1817 he entitled a poem 'On Sitting Down to Read *King Lear* Once Again'.

In the last days of 1623, the First Folio, a bumper book of Shakespeare plays, was for sale in St Paul's Churchyard. A boy at St Paul's School nearby, John Milton, had just turned 16. He was a keen reader: 'After I was 12 years old,' he later recalled, 'I rarely retired to bed from my studies till midnight.' Milton read the First

Folio, and contributed a sonnet to the Second Folio of 1632. This, his first published poem, begins: 'What needs my Shakespeare for his honoured bones ...' In headlining the words 'my Shakespeare', Milton recalled Ben Jonson, who had proudly written 'my ... Shakespeare' three times in his famous poem in the First Folio. Milton was well aware that Jonson had known Shakespeare personally, whereas he, Milton, knew Shakespeare through reading. His sonnet testifies devoutly to the 'deep impression' left on him by his Shakespeare's 'Delphick lines'. The teenage Milton may have been the youngest person to have come to know Shakespeare chiefly by reading the plays, though his poems 'L'Allegro' and 'Il Penseroso' suggest that he attended plays by Jonson and Shakespeare. The theatre records for the years 1623 to 1642 are patchy but they do not show Shakespeare revivals as prominent; not all his plays will have been put on. But the 1623 Folio made Shakespeare's drama available as a whole, for reading and rereading. We missed the performances of 400 years ago, but, thanks to the Folio, the plays are still with us.

Reading Shakespeare looks at half of the surviving plays, and at the Sonnets. It is written throughout on the assumption that the reader's curiosity about Shakespeare is not confined to a single play about to be studied or seen. The book is so ordered as to be read as a whole, in the hope of enabling, at a modest level, an idea of the shape of Shakespeare's writing career. Accordingly, discussions of single plays are not self-contained but vary in length and approach, purposely avoiding a standard formula. Some go into detail; others will summarise a story or explore a specific theme or an aspect of more general relevance. Plot summary is sometimes necessary, though it flattens and simplifies, as all commentary does. In the case of a play not yet read, reading a sketch of its story helps build a larger idea of Shakespeare. General topics are likewise handled in the introductory sections, but reappear later. What is said on language, and of verse, follows the account of Shakespeare's earliest plays. A reader who wants to get the most out of this book is strongly advised to use both the Contents and the Index, which lists topics as well as the titles of plays.

Reading Shakespeare begins with a sketch of Shakespeare's life and work, then looks more closely at 20 plays, though with varying degrees of fullness, and at the Sonnets. Nearly everything

Shakespeare wrote gets a mention, since a sense of the order of composition of his work helps in understanding each part of it. Some of this information is also given in tables and chronological lists.

Most readers of this book are likely to have met Shakespeare by reading a play in an English class at school. His work survived because it was printed. It lives on the page as well as on the stage, and to be fully understood it has to be read as well as seen. This introduction is addressed primarily to those whose access to his work, however often they may now see it performed on stage or screen, has been nourished by reading and imagining it. 'In recent years, it has become all the more necessary to read William Shakespeare. We live in a visual, rather than an oral, culture.'[3]

Shakespeare remains central to the idea and practice of English as a university subject, although there are now degree courses in the subject where he is the only required author from before 1800 or even later, which makes it hard to see him historically. Specialisation ('research') rules in universities, and lecturers on Shakespeare are often specialists. Specialists are useful but can be territorial; and Shakespeare does not belong to specialists, or to academics, or to directors, but to audiences and readers.

Why add a pebble to the pyramid of books piled on Shakespeare? Because, in a specialising age, I believe that what many students of English need, and some might appreciate, is a modest and fairly basic introduction to reading his work. The primary aim of the book, it should be made clear, is to facilitate the reading of Shakespeare, not to offer a guide to current commentary on his work.

As Samuel Johnson put it in the Preface to his edition of Shakespeare's Plays (1765), 'Let him that is yet unacquainted with the powers of Shakespeare, and who desired to feel the highest pleasure that the drama can give, read every play from the first scene to the last, with utter negligence of all his commentators.'[4]

Acknowledgements

Anyone who writes on Shakespeare writes by reflected light. It would seem odd to thank Jonson or Johnson, or to select from among their many successors, so I record thanks here only to those who helped directly: Barbara Murray and Andrew Murphy at St Andrews, and more especially Neil Rhodes. Emma Smith of Oxford very kindly read through the manuscript of a new acquaintance, reducing the number of my errors. My thanks to Mary Alexander for patient support, and much more; to Jenna Steventon, an encouraging editor; and to the Glaswegians who long ago cast me as Bottom.

The editor and publishers wish to thank the following for permission to reproduce copyright material:

British Library for extract from Addition (D) to *Sir Thomas More*, © The British Library Board, All Rights Reserved, MS Harley 7368, folio 9; Cambridge University Press for image and text from K. Muir and S. Schoenbaum (ed.) *New Companion to Shakespeare* (1971); Folger Shakespeare Library for image from *[Works, 1623] Mr. William Shakespeare's comedies, histories, & tragedies:* Catalogue of Plays, Call no. STC 22273 Fo.1 No. 68, image *from Shakespeare's Hamlet/*facsimilied from the edition printed at London in 1603, facsimile Q1 (1603) title page, Call No. PR2752 1861–1871 Sh.Col. No. 26, image from *Shakespeare's Hamlet/*facsimilied from the edition printed at London in 1604, facsimile Q2 (1604) title page, PR2752 1861–1871 Sh.Col. No. 27, by permission of the Folger Shakespeare Library; Heritage Images for the title page of the First Folio, with portrait engraved by Martin Droeshout, Ann Ronan Picture Library/Heritage Images, and *Long View of London* (1641) by Wenceslaus Hallar, City of London/Heritage Images, © www.Heritage-Images.com; TopFoto for image of Stratford Grammar School, © 2005 TopFoto, TopFoto.co.uk;

Utrecht University Library for image from Utrecht University Library Ms. 842, fol. 132r.

Every effort has been made to trace rights holders, but if any have been inadvertently overlooked the publishers would be pleased to make the necessary arrangements at the first opportunity.

1
First Things

Reading Shakespeare is written for anyone studying William Shakespeare or simply reading some part of his work. It addresses Shakespeare and his writing career as directly as it can. Yet he is not a simple writer, and aspects of his work are no longer familiar. He wrote in verse, the normal medium for plays in his day, and verse was expected to display a certain eloquence, though Shakespeare soon varied his style, and also introduced prose. English itself has changed over four centuries, making some features of Elizabethan English unfamiliar; yet we can understand Shakespeare's adventurous language and read it with enjoyment. Human lives have also changed a great deal in these centuries, as have our ideas of human nature; but Shakespeare's understanding of life remains strikingly valuable. This human understanding was what Samuel Johnson valued most in him. Dr Johnson's conclusion, in the Preface to his edition of the plays of Shakespeare, was that from reading his work 'a hermit may estimate the transactions of the world, and a confessor predict the progress of the passions'.[1] Few hermits or confessors will pick up this book, but many contemporary readers are able to say that some of their most pleasant and vivid learning about the possibilities of human life has come to them through their experience of Shakespeare's plays.

William Shakespeare lived from 1564 to 1616. He was for 20 of those years a noted poet, and was soon recognised as the leading playwright of Queen Elizabeth's last decade and of the first decade of the reign of King James. But it was not an age of memoirs, and we know next to nothing about him of a strictly personal kind. We have official records of his baptism and marriage, of family christenings and family deaths. We also have London theatre records and several records from Stratford-upon-Avon of financial, legal and property dealings. We can draw a line to link up these official points, but inside this outline there is little to reveal what sort of person the unofficial Shakespeare was: there are six signatures on legal documents, a draft of a scene for a play which did not reach the stage, but not a single letter from him. He appeared once as a witness in a court case, but his testimony is carefully non-committal. His contemporaries admired Shakespeare the writer, but we have no first-hand impression of Shakespeare the man: nothing composed in his lifetime; no undisputed lifetime portrait; an uninspired bust on his tomb in Stratford; and a pleasant commemorative engraving, also post-humous. This portrait engraving is a good likeness, according to Ben Jonson's verse 'To the Reader', which faces the portrait at the front of the large collected edition of Shakespeare plays published in 1623, known as the First Folio (Illustration 1).

Ben Jonson's advice to the reader, however, is to 'looke, / Not on his Picture, but his Booke'. The poem is reproduced below. The book's title is *Mr William Shakespeares Comedies, Histories, & Tragedies, Published according to the True Originall Copies*, a bumper book of 36 plays (see Illustration 2 on p. 4). The Folio is the sole text for half of the plays and the base text for some others. Shakespeare also collaborated with John Fletcher in the writing of three further plays. Apart from 'his Booke' of plays, three small books of Shakespeare's verse also survive.

To the Reader

The Figure, that thou here seest put,
   It was for gentle Shakespeare cut,
Wherein the Graver had a strife
   With Nature, to out-dooe the life;
O, could he but have drawn his Wit
   As well in brasse as he hath hit

His face, the Print would then
            surpasse
All, that was ever writ in brasse.
But since he cannot, Reader, looke
   Not on his Picture, but his Booke.

BEN JONSON

Illustration 1 Portrait of Shakespeare on the title page of the First Folio (1623), engraved by Martin Droeshout – the first portrait of an English author to have been used on the title page of his works. Jonson says, in verses facing the portrait, that it was a good likeness, so it is the nearest thing we have to a likeness. But it is unlikely to have been done from life, since Droeshout was born in 1601

A CATALOGVE

of the feuerall Comedies, Histories, and Tragedies contained in this Volume.

COMEDIES.

THe Tempeft.	Folio 1.
The two Gentlemen of Verona.	20
The Merry Wiues of Windfor.	38
Meafure for Meafure.	61
The Comedy of Errours.	85
Much adoo about Nothing.	101
Loues Labour loft.	122
Midfommer Nights Dreame.	145
The Merchant of Venice.	163
As you Like it.	185
The Taming of the Shrew.	208
All is well, that Ends well.	230
Twelfe-Night, or what you will.	255
The Winters Tale.	304

HISTORIES.

The Life and Death of King John.	Fol. 1.
The Life & death of Richard the fecond.	23
The Firft part of King Henry the fourth.	46
The Second part of K. Henry the fourth.	74
The Life of King Henry the Fift.	69
The Firft part of King Henry the Sixt.	96
The Second part of King Hen. the Sixt.	120
The Third part of King Henry the Sixt.	147
The Life & Death of Richard the Third.	173
The Life of King Henry the Eight.	205

TRAGEDIES.

The Tragedy of Coriolanus.	Fol. 1.
Titus Andronicus.	31
Romeo and Juliet.	53
Timon of Athens.	80
The Life and death of Julius Cæfar.	109
The Tragedy of Macbeth.	131
The Tragedy of Hamlet.	152
King Lear.	283
Othello, the Moore of Venice.	310
Anthony and Cleopater.	346
Cymbeline King of Britaine.	369

Illustration 2 The Table of Contents of the First Folio (1623) catalogues the plays by genre, a decision which makes genre seem Shakespeare's priority, which was not always the case. *Cymbeline* appears as a tragedy. *Pericles* and *The Two Noble Kinsmen*, collaboratively written plays, are omitted. By permission of the Folger Shakespeare Library

Career in brief

The known facts of Shakespeare's life are few. Born in 1564, he married young and at 20 was the father of three children. The first note of him as a writer came in a rival's scornful attack. In 1592, Robert Greene, a graduate of both Cambridge and Oxford, a prolific writer and a talented rogue, was dying, aged 34. His last work, *Greene's Groatsworth of Wit, Bought with a Million of Repentance*, warned his fellow University Wits against Christopher Marlowe, and also against an actor, 'a puppet ... an upstart crow, beautified with our feathers, that ... supposes he is as well able to bombast out a blank verse as the best of you: and being an absolute *Johannes fac totum* [Jack of all trades], is in his own conceit the only Shake-scene in a country.'[2]

Robert Greene's deathbed fears proved prophetic. Greene's 'puppet' could indeed fill out a line of blank verse, and the *fac totum* could indeed 'do everything' in the theatre, write as well as act. Shakespeare, then aged 28, had certainly learned from the work of the University Wits – Lyly, Marlowe, Peele, Lodge, Nashe, and Greene himself – and knew how to write a play. By 1594 he was the leading Shake-scene in England. In the year of Greene's death, 1592, the theatres closed, as bubonic plague killed one in ten of London's 200,000 people. In 1593 and 1594 death removed the two leading tragic dramatists, but not by disease: Thomas Kyd died after torture by the authorities; his associate Christopher Marlowe was killed in an obscure brawl in a tavern, possibly a political murder. At the same time, John Lyly gave up writing his fashionable comedies, despairing of Queen Elizabeth's stingy patronage. In these two years Shakespeare completed and published two acclaimed long poems. So by the time the theatres reopened in 1594, Greene's 'puppet' and 'upstart crow' was a recognised poet. The first work to which he attached his name, and by which he made his name, was *Venus and Adonis*, 1593. This was followed by (*The Rape of*) *Lucrece*, 1594.[3] These are accomplished and sophisticated poems, one comic, the other tragic, each of well over a thousand lines, recounting erotic episodes from classical literature in a smoothly artificial verse. They are largely composed of oratorical speeches of seduction, but these eloquent persuasions do not persuade the person to whom they are addressed. Venus does not persuade Adonis; Tarquin does not persuade Lucrece; Lucrece does not persuade Tarquin. These elegantly printed poems were immediately successful, reprinting far more often than any of his plays, and were presumably rewarded by their dedicatee, the Earl of Southampton. At 30, Shakespeare was famous as a poet. He seems, however, to have decided at this point that his future as a writer lay in the commercial theatre in which he had started.

The plays he wrote from 1595 onward show an advance on his earlier work. For the next 20 years he was the leading playwright, providing his company with about two plays a year until 1603, then about one a year until 1610, when he spent more time in Stratford, leaving Ben Jonson as his leading successor among the many writers for the stage. Shakespeare had completed his poems at the right moment. 'There is a tide in the affairs of men,' says Brutus in *Julius Caesar*, 'which, taken at the flood, leads on to fortune' (4.3.218–19). Just at the moment Greene, Kyd, Marlowe and Lyly were taken from the race, Shakespeare hit his stride as a playwright. His work shows intelligence, eloquence, ambition and knowledge of the theatre. But he also had good timing. Printed discussion of politics was under state control, as was the Church of England. If religious subjects were not allowed on the stage, other issues could be ventilated there, as long as nothing was too identifiable. Shakespeare joined the London theatre as it became very popular indeed, at all levels of society. Theatre was, more than Parliament, the Church or the press, a major outlet of conscious cultural activity. It had a kind of unofficial public monopoly, and players became, as Hamlet says, 'the abstract and brief chronicles of the time' (2.2.520).

Authorship

What Shakespeare has left us, his writings, are all we have of him. It should be enough. A growing cult of Shakespeare, however, created a wish to know more: to gain an intimate sense of what he was like. This wish cannot be satisfied. Its frustration has led to some odd reactions, the most perverse of which is to distrust the documentary record and to choose to believe, instead, that the works printed with Shakespeare's name on the title page were not written by him. The records offer no reason to doubt that William Shakespeare of Stratford-upon-Avon wrote the poems and the plays published over his name in his lifetime, or that he wrote the plays collected in the Folio edition that were published as his work by two of his fellows in the King's Men after his death, a publication strongly endorsed by his friend and rival Ben Jonson. The contemporary record is unanimous in saying that Shakespeare wrote these works; no contemporary hints that he did not. Something – as little as possible – has to be said about what is sometimes called the authorship controversy.

The spaces between the recorded facts of William Shakespeare's life have been filled in with tradition, legend, intelligent speculation and headlong fantasy. The actor-poet-playwright Ben Jonson knew Shakespeare well: Shakespeare had acted in Jonson's plays. Jonson wrote that 'he loved the man, this side Idolatry'. The mention of idolatry has proved prophetic. Actors can become idols, but veneration of Shakespeare as the national poet was recommended to a wider world at the so-called Jubilee celebrations at Stratford in 1769. These were organised by the Scottish writer James Boswell, admirer and biographer of Dr Johnson, and one of the first celebrators of celebrity. At this publicity event the actor David Garrick, for whom Shakespeare was already a goldmine, read a poem ending "tis he, 'tis he, / The God of our idolatry'. It was now that Shakespeare was first dubbed 'the Bard'. Advanced opinion in the 1760s was fascinated by bards, the professional oral poets of Welsh pre-history, about whom almost nothing was known. Calling the poet 'the Bard' expressed a proto-Romantic awe for a supposedly untutored primitive genius emerging from a period of Britain's history about which little was then known. Shakespeare was a poet as well as a dramatist, and all poetry is 'oral' in that its words are to be spoken. But 'Bard' is an odd title for a poet who was not oral but literate, not Welsh but English, writing for a commercial theatre in south London. Scholars do not speak seriously of 'the Bard', though they sometimes use the word 'Bardolatry', a word coined by George Bernard Shaw.

Samuel Johnson, a friend of both Garrick and Boswell, was devoted to Shakespeare but not an idolator. His *Preface to Shakespeare*, a fount of commonsense, is quoted more than once in this book as it is the last major pre-academic account of Shakespeare before worship became general. Johnson admires but feels free to criticise.

An amusing instance of how far the cult of Shakespeare had spread, and of how older reservations lingered, is recorded in the memoirs of the novelist Fanny Burney, which record her conversation with King George III on 19 December 1785:

> 'Was there ever,' cried he, 'such stuff as a great part of Shakespeare! But one must not say so! But what think you? – Is there not sad stuff? What? – What?'
>
> 'Yes, indeed, I think so, sir, though mixed with such excellencies that –'
>
> 'Oh!' cried he, laughing good-humouredly, 'I know it is not to be said! But it's true. Only it's Shakespeare, and nobody dare abuse him.' Then he enumerated many of the characters and parts of plays that he objected to; and when he had run them over, finished with again laughing and exclaiming, 'But one should be stoned for saying so.'[4]

From the 1760s onward, Shakespeare's reputation rose and rose and became international; German Romantic critics exalted him above the French neoclassical drama of Racine and Corneille. His natural talent is unaccountable, and it seemed strange to Bardolaters that such quasi-divine works could have been written by a man of no known education – the son, it was discovered, of parents who did not sign their names. It was also found that he had invested his London earnings in property in and around the very small Midlands town where his father had been a glover; and that he went to law to protect his financial interests. So Shakespeare was more like an ordinary man than a bard. But he never had been a bard, and a common man can have uncommon talent. Extraordinary things are often done by people from ordinary backgrounds: among English writers one might instance John Keats and Charles Dickens. Snobbery aside, there is a fundamental error in this line of thinking: the unimaginative assumption that authors can write only of what they have personally experienced. Yet no one has ever supposed that the author of these plays had met Cleopatra, or Cymbeline, King of Britain, or even King Henry V. One does not have to have visited Italy in order to set a play in Verona. But Bardolatry interacted with an unthinking assumption about where writers get their material from to produce the conclusion that the plays published in Shakespeare's name could not have been written by him. Surely the author of such great works must have been a great man: well educated, travelled, familiar with courts. Why not a lord who did not want to be known to scribble for the public stage and used the Stratford player as his cover? An American, Delia Bacon, proposed in the 1850s that the true Bard was the Chancellor of England, Francis Bacon. When read, however, Lord Bacon's writings show that he could not have written plays of this kind, and the Chancellor was eventually put back in his box. A devout believer in Bacon was the American comic writer Samuel Clemens, who himself wrote under an assumed name, Mark Twain. The current favourite for the true author of 'Shakespeare' is the seventeenth Earl of Oxford, who, dying in 1604, kindly left ten further plays in his bottom drawer, to appear later over the name of the Stratford player. The Viennese psychoanalyst Sigmund Freud, a decoder of dreams, was an obstinate believer in Lord Oxford. The idea that 'Shakespeare' was written by someone else is a fantasy which appeals to a taste for conspiratorial explanation – and to those who exploit that taste. It has no other merit. A number of Shakespearian actors are positive that Shakespeare's works could not possibly have been written by an actor. But there is no reason to doubt that they were.[5]

Play and page

A playwright writes a script for performance. This playwright wrote unusually well, but, as was pointed out by Aristotle in his analysis of literature known as the *Poetics*, language is only one component of drama. Other components, as Shakespeare knew better than Aristotle, are the players themselves, singly and in groups. Their faces, voices, bodies, costumes, gestures and moves enact the unfolding of the action. Then there is the theatre itself, its acting space, and any scenery, lighting and stage props, and its auditorium. An audience is also required, for without the ears, eyes and minds of an audience, a play is not really a play. The fundamental premise of this book, however, is that a single reader fully counts as an audience. Finally, there is what Aristotle calls the action, the story enacted. His own chief interest was in the unfolding of the action of tragedy, and in its social function.

To these basics, Shakespeare often adds music, song and dance, and sometimes a dumb show, pageant or masque.

Four centuries after Shakespeare signed his will, all we have is a set of printed versions of his scripts: sequences of dialogues, speeches and stage directions. The company of the King's Men and the houses in which they played are gone. In 1642 the public theatres were closed by Parliament and kept closed by Lord Protector Cromwell. The closure was not total, but the performing traditions of the King's Men were largely lost by 1660, when theatres of a new kind were being built, with proscenium arches, and new kinds of plays put on by new companies. Half of the plays of Shakespeare survive only because two of his colleagues in the King's Men collected and edited them, printing them in 1623. Before 1623, performance preceded print, just as composition had preceded performance. After 1660 performance derived from print. If the King James version of the Bible of 1611 had not happened, there were other English Bibles to refer to. But without the Folio of 1623 we would have only half of Shakespeare's plays.

Plays are written to be performed. Can reading, then, be as valid an experience of drama as attending a stage performance? The answer is 'Yes, it can', for reading and performing are not opposites but different parts of the one process. Each needs the other. A theatrical performance of a play begins in a reading. In contemporary practice, a director reads the script, there is a cast 'read-through', and parts are learned by reading them again and again. Equally, a silent solo reading of a play involves performance: the reader both imagines a performance of the play and receives it in the mind; each speech has to be 'produced', heard and seen, by an inward ear and eye; each speaker placed on a mental stage.

Dr Johnson took the literary view of drama to its logical extreme, pronouncing that 'A play read affects the mind like a play acted' and, more severely, 'A dramatic exhibition is a book recited with concomitants that increase or diminish its effect.'[6] Before dismissing Johnson's provocative statement we should first recall that Johnson, like Shakespeare and Milton before him, had a formal education rooted in reading Latin texts: construing them with concentration and care, and also, since all three men were poets, with imagination. For such readers, for whom literature in 'dead' languages was alive, the page was no less living than the stage.

To a mind thus trained, the 'effect' of reading was as vivid as physical performance. Milton and Johnson might have regarded the 'concomitants' of the theatre as distracting accidentals. The same is true for readers with less linguistic training but a strong response to language and to verse – for John Keats, for example.[7]

Can reading match performance? A reader of a play who sees performances can compare instances, and an experienced reader can imagine a performance better than some of those that are staged. A good mental performance is also available to a less experienced reader sensitive to language and capable of imagining action. Actual performances usually fall short of perfection, through faults in conception or execution. In performance, Shakespeare's longest texts, such as *King Lear* or the long versions of *Hamlet*, are nearly always abridged. Irrecoverable jokes are cut, and verbal details are altered for cultural reasons. Juliet's age, for example, can be changed from 13 to 18; Shylock's 'I hate him for he is a Christian' can be cut. In cases such as these, the reader of a full text has everything that Shakespeare wrote (or as close as we can get to this), not a cut-down text or one doctored for cultural reasons. It is also possible that he, or she, can offer a mental performance of its action superior in some ways to that of a theatre company under inept or cranky direction. There are productions of *Macbeth* in which Seton, a minor character, is made into a figure of Satan. Performance and reading illuminate each other. This is not to deny the indispensability of stage performance, nor the life and power of physical enactment, nor the grace and skill of good ensemble performance, an experience with dimensions which no solo reader can fully imagine. I write as one who has acted and who likes acting. But directors can misconceive plays, and misdirection matters more than faulty acting. I also write as one who has read thousands of essays on Shakespeare and knows that readings of a play can be sadly inadequate.

Anyone who regularly sees Shakespeare, even in the most approved theatres, has seen performances that fall well short of the ideal. Imperfect acting is a subject which Shakespeare explicitly asks audiences to consider. Prologues and Epilogues, and indeed his characters, discuss it. Theseus says of some bad acting in *A Midsummer Night's Dream* that 'the best in this kind are but shadows' (players were sometimes called 'shadows'). Hamlet himself discusses good acting at discerning length. Characters also observe that human beings themselves act so badly that the gods laugh or the angels weep. Generally, when the characters discuss inept acting, or a Prologue discusses the physical limitations of the theatre (as happens several times in *Henry V*), Shakespeare will remind the audience to use their imaginations. Bad acting, then, is shown and discussed on stage. But mistaken production is not discussed in the same way. This author wrote and acted in his plays; he was a partner in the company and shared in its profits. He may have acted less often towards the end of his career, but he was involved in the producing of his plays. Not once does he raise the possibility that a professional production might be conceived on mistaken assumptions.

Shakespeare wrote to be performed, but his plays were also read. Half of them were published in his lifetime, and from 1623 his collected plays could be read as a whole. He often says in his Sonnets that he expects to be read. Indeed his sonnets claim that they will be remembered when all other means to lasting remembrance, such as monuments in stone or bronze, have failed. He claims that his poems will last until the Day of Judgement, when time will end. Sonnet 18, 'When I compare thee to a summer's day', brags that 'So long as men can breathe and eyes can see, / So long lives this, and this gives life to thee.' 'This' will be read for as long as men have eyes to read a poem and breath to read a poem aloud. Poems today are not read aloud as often as they used to be, but literary immortality was an explicit aim of the verse which Shakespeare composed for the page, and the record suggests that it was also an aim of his writing for the stage; an aim less consistent and, for reasons of genre, less explicit. Even an immodest playwright – George Bernard Shaw, for example – does not explicitly claim that his drama will last for all time.[8]

Such a claim was made explicitly by Ben Jonson for *Mr William Shakespeare's Comedies, Histories and Tragedies* in the remarkable poem which prefaces the First Folio, the collected edition of 1623. In this, the first substantial assessment of Shakespeare, Jonson ranks him as the best playwright produced by Europe either in classical antiquity or since, declaring of this 'Star of poets' that 'He was not of an age but for all time.'[9] Jonson's achievements and critical acumen qualify him to judge Shakespeare's work and worth. The 'for all time' judgement was supported by subsequent poets and dramatists: Milton, Dryden, Pope, Johnson, Coleridge, Arnold and Eliot. For three centuries, writers of this calibre were the leading commentators on Shakespeare, and Pope and Johnson also edited the complete plays. In the nineteenth century, however, major editions of Shakespeare were made not by poets but by scholars; in the twentieth, by professional scholars in universities. Editors have become the top dogs among professional academic experts on Shakespeare, and writing on his work has increasingly been obliged to take account of the rise of the editor, for reasons now to be mentioned.

Printed books

Shakespeare survives in printed books. Of the thousands of pages he covered in ink, all we now have of his own handwriting is what is generally accepted as his draft of a three-page scene written for *Sir Thomas More*, a multi-authored play which did not reach the stage and was not printed (Illustration 3). Experts on Elizabethan handwriting generally accept that Shakespeare's six surviving signatures, some in abbreviated form, are in the same hand as this draft. Each signature is slightly different in its spelling (spelling was phonetic and unstandardised), and the version in which we know his name, 'Shakespeare', is not one of them: 'Willm Shaksp; William Shaespe; Wm Shakespe; William Shakspere; Willm Shakspere; William Shakspeare'. Three of these are on his will, the last, shakily: 'By me, William Shakspeare'. Had *Sir Thomas More* been printed, we could have compared the handwritten draft with a printed text. But we cannot do so. We do not even have a line of Shakespeare in the hand of a copyist. How, then, can we know that the printed texts that we have are close to Shakespeare's texts? A crevasse of doubt opens up. Scholars believe that some of the plays are printed from finally approved texts, but that others are not. The texts we have are, however, all we have. Making a leap of faith – or not seeing the crevasse – we step across and read the edited texts. There is no alternative.

Scholars of handwriting, theatre history and printing practice have studied the operations by which a text passed from authorial manuscript(s) to theatre copies to printer's copy to printed book; and the kinds of error likely at each stage. Such knowledge helps when

what Country by the nature of yor error
fhoold gyve you harber go yo^u to ffraunc or flanders
to any Jarman pvince, ~~to~~ fpane or portigall
nay any where ~~why yo~~^u that not adheres to Ingland
why yo^u muft neede be ftraingers, woold yo^u be pleafd
to find a nation of fuch barbarous temper
that breaking out in hiddious violence
woold not afoord yo^u, an abode on earth
whett their detefted knyves againft yor throtes
fpurne yo^u lyke dogge, and lyke as yf that god
owed not nor made not yo^u, nor that the elamente

              yor
wer not all appropriat to ~~their~~ Comforte.
but Charterd vnto them, what woold yo^u thinck
to be thus vfd, this is the ftraingers cafe
and this your momtanifh inhumanyty

Illustration 3 Lines 126–40 of Addition (D) to *Sir Thomas More*, Shakespeare's hand, with transcription below. More speaks to calm Londoners rioting against Flemish immigrants. The draft seems rapidly written, with deletions and false starts. The verse is unlineated. Spelling, punctuation and capitalisation are inconsistent. The modern spelling of words occurring in unfamiliar forms in the transcription is (in text order): should, harbour, France, German, Spain, needs, pleased, whet, dogs, if, God, owned, used, case, Mahometanish (= Muslim). The play did not get past the censor. © The British Library Board, All Rights Reserved, MS Harley 7368, folio 9.

printed texts diverge, as they usually do – sometimes drastically. A Quarto was the equivalent of a modern paperback, and typically cost sixpence, whereas the First Folio, a very large format volume, cost 40 times as much, one pound sterling, before it was bound in calf. (The format terms refer to the number of times the sheet of paper is folded before printing. A Folio is folded once, making two leaves, four large pages; Folio is Italian for leaf, modern Italian *foglio*. *Quarto* is Italian for four: a Quarto has four leaves, made by folding the sheet twice, to make eight squarish pages.) The first Quarto of *Hamlet*, for example, an unauthorised version pirated for acting purposes, has about 2200 lines; the second Quarto text has about 3800 lines (see Illustrations 7 and 8, pp. 102–3). This second Quarto is the basis of the Folio text, which, however, is 230 lines shorter and has many differences. Editors choose one of the longer versions as a base text, but difficult decisions remain, as for example when the text cannot be made to make sense, when error is evident, or when texts differ. An editor needs to know about handwriting, printing, general linguistic usage, Shakespeare's own usage and spelling, other plays of the time, and Elizabethan and Jacobean theatrical, literary and historical contexts. Beginners, however, simply read the modernised and tidied-up text without giving a thought to its editor. Nor need they. Undergraduates may hear about textual scholarship, but it is usually passed over as a matter for specialists. And so it is, but these specialists decide the texts.

Editors aim at giving us what Shakespeare wrote, but for theatre directors, a text is a recipe or set of prompts for a production. The attitude of the theatre to a script is, first, to make it work; and, if necessary, to adapt the text by rewriting, cutting, updating. Respect for the text was not a general rule in productions of Shakespeare before the twentieth century, when it became more of a consideration. In earlier centuries, tragedy could be rewritten as comedy: *King Lear* was presented between 1681 and 1845, in the adaptation of Nahum Tate, with a happy ending in which virtue is rewarded and Cordelia marries Edgar. Comedy could be cut to make tragedy: Henry Irving's celebrated 1873 *Merchant of Venice* brought down the final curtain on the exit of the defeated Shylock at the end of Act 4, omitting the whole of Act 5 and its marital reunions. Since 1623, and even today, someone who wants to get at what Shakespeare wrote has to read him. And those who do not read a play before seeing it will miss a great deal. At school, as in the theatre, we get our Shakespeare play by play. But a complete Shakespeare enables a reader, by comparing play with play, to understand them better. Even to read an account of half of his plays can help.

Posthumous publication

A last feature of the printing of Shakespeare deserves mention before we turn to his life and writings. John Heminges and Henry Condell prefaced their Folio edition of Shakespeare's plays, 1623, with an epistle 'To the Great Variety of Readers', a variety which ran 'from the most able to him that can but spell'. They regret that Shakespeare did not oversee the texts:

> It had been a thing, we confess, worthy to have been wished that the author himself had lived to have set forth and overseen his own writings. But since it hath been ordained otherwise, and he by death departed from that right, we pray you do not envy his friends the office of their care and pain to have collected and published them ...[10]

Editors in the eighteenth century found that some of the plays in the Folio had already appeared in Quarto, but that others had not. Among the 18 plays first printed in the Folio are *Twelfth Night*, *The Tempest*, *Macbeth* and *Antony and Cleopatra*. Why should plays such as these have been previously unprinted? It is now thought that five out of six of *all* plays of this period have disappeared, but from 1594, when the theatre reopened, new plays by Shakespeare were normally put into Quarto. The company 'regarded publication of his plays as conducive, rather than prejudicial, to their commercial success in the playhouse'.[11] However, after 1602 new Shakespeare plays were not usually put into Quarto. This is often explained by saying that printing a play would have allowed other companies to perform it, reducing receipts. Perhaps, but we do not know enough to say that either of these opposite explanations is conclusive. Alexander Pope, believing that the reason for non-publication was commercial, exclaims, in his imitation of an epistle by the Roman poet Horace, that

> Shakespear, (whom you and ev'ry Play-house bill
> Style the divine, the matchless, what you will)

> For gain, not glory, wing'd his roving flight,
> And grew Immortal in his own despight.[12]

Pope himself had – for gain as well as glory – edited all Shakespeare's plays. Confronted by texts lacking a consistent verbal finish, Pope used typography to mark their 'blemishes' and 'beauties'.[13] Ben Jonson had found Shakespeare careless, and Milton had cast 'Sweetest Shakespeare' as 'Nature's child / Warbling his native woodnotes wild', hence Pope's idea of Shakespeare as a natural prodigy who dashed off things for the stage, caring little either for his texts or for his literary afterlife.[14] Dr Johnson lent weight to this view, concluding that Shakespeare was 'careless of future fame.... When his plays had been acted, his hope was at an end; he solicited no addition of honour from the reader.'[15]

The idea that Shakespeare did not care whether his plays were read derives not just from the difference between a play and a poem but from a long-accepted inference from the non-publication of these later plays in his lifetime. Jonson arranged for his own work to be handsomely printed and Shakespeare did not; but an inference from a negative is not certain. Horace had advised other Roman poets to 'keep your piece nine years' before making them public. Alexander Pope in his 'Epistle to Arbuthnot' repeats this advice to aspirant poets as 'keep your piece nine years' –meaning also 'keep your peace nine years: desist, be silent, do not trouble us with your scribbling.' Yet if Pope had written *Antony and Cleopatra*, we may be certain that he would not have left it nine years in a bottom drawer. Pope simply could not understand how that piece, and 17 others, could be kept for so long and be published only posthumously.

Pope was not aware that Shakespeare's scripts belonged not to him but to the King's Men, though presumably each sharer got a cut of the receipts. Two of the company, Heminges and Condell, explain that they collected and printed their colleague's plays as a labour of love. In his will, Shakespeare gave memorial rings to three of his fellows in the company: to its leader and leading player Richard Burbage, to Heminges, and to Condell. He wished to be remembered by two colleagues who were already, so it seems, making sure that he would be remembered. The 1623 Folio has all the plays of which he was sole or principal author, both those that had previously appeared in Quarto and those that had not.

The pattern of publication of the plays deserves a further look. After Shakespeare had made his name as a poet, new plays written between 1594 and 1602 were normally printed in single Quartos two years after performance. He was a widely published author, the most widely published dramatist of his day. His name sold plays. Over 50 editions of plays and poems by Shakespeare appeared before the Folio of 1623. But the pattern changed. After the second Quarto of *Hamlet*, 1603, only three new plays went into print before Shakespeare's death in 1616. The title page of the second *Hamlet* Quarto reads, 'Newly imprinted and enlarged to almost as much againe as it was, according to the true and perfect Coppie'. (See Illustrations 7 and 8 on pp. 102–3.) Shakespeare's company wanted their text to be accurately printed according to the 'perfect Coppie': in its perfected final state. A 'perfect' text was, then, a matter of importance – especially if an unauthorised text of such a play had appeared. Ben Jonson's elegant *Works* had appeared in 1616, the year of Shakespeare's death. Within three years, two printers, Pavier and Jaggard, embarked on reprinting ten Shakespeare plays in Quarto. The King's Men acted to suppress this scheme. They had in mind a greater scheme, perhaps long contemplated, to collect all the plays (including early plays never printed) for a grand edition, dedicated to the Earl of Pembroke and his brother. Securing 'the True Originall Copies', ordering them and printing them 'according to' those copies took some years. Delays in the arrival of the Folio are not evidence that the dead author did not care whether he was read.

These preliminaries have been necessary so that we are aware of the relations between a script and a play, and between a play and its printed afterlife. Modern texts of Shakespeare are the result of generations of editing. Editing the play-texts from their first printings is not easy, but for some time it proceeded on the basis that the finally edited text could take promising readings from all suitable early texts. This editorial consensus broke up in the 1980s, at the same time as a new focus on performance was developed. In a taught course of English literature, the texts of the plays are the basis for the study of Shakespeare, but we should approach his texts in a more conscious awareness of how they can be arrived at. We can now turn to the man and his work.

2
The Recorded Life

William Shakespeare's name first appears on 26 April 1564, in the baptismal record of the parish church of Stratford-upon-Avon, Holy Trinity. Holy Trinity is a grand medieval church for a small south Midlands market town of 2000-odd inhabitants. Stratford, sited at a crossing of the River Avon, which flows westward to meet the River Severn, is a day's ride from Oxford; and Oxford to London is a two-day ride along the valley of the Thames. The register entry reads: *'Guglielmus filius Johannes Shakspere'*. He must have attended Stratford school; the pupil lists are lost. The details of when he left school, and where and how he lived before and after his marriage, are unknown. He next appears at 18 as 'William Shagspere', marrying 'Anne Hathwey', and then at the baptism of their daughter Susanna in 1583, and of their twins, Judith and Hamnet, in 1585. At the age of 20, Shakespeare had a wife and three children; he needed to make money. By 1592 his success as a playwright had drawn Robert Greene's printed attack on him as an upstart, a 'Shake-scene', a player who presumed to *write* plays.

After 1592 his name is found in records of family marriages and deaths, in theatre records and in property and financial trans-actions. There is no information of a personal or private kind. A letter asking Shakespeare for a loan survives, but the letter was not sent. We have addresses where he lodged in London. His recorded evidence in a court case is non-committal. Such contemporary comment on him as there is, is polite, friendly, general.

As a writer, however, his reputation was soon established. In 1598, *Palladis Tamia or Wit's Treasury*, a 'Comparative Discourse of our

English poets with the Greeke, Latin, and Italian poets', which was a survey of 80 writers on the London literary scene by an up-to-date young cleric, Francis Meres, put Shakespeare top in comedy and tragedy: 'As Plautus and Seneca are accounted the best for Comedy and Tragedy among the Latines: so Shake-speare among the English is the most excellent in both kinds for the stage; for Comedy, witnes his Gentlemen of Verona, his Errors, his Love labours lost, his Love labours wonne, his Midsummers night dream, & his Merchant of Venice: for Tragedy his Richard the 2. Richard the 3. Henry the 4. King Iohn, Titus Andronicus and his Romeo and Juliet.' Meres also mentions his 'sugared Sonnets among his private friends'.[1] Shakespeare and Chapman are for Meres poets by whom 'the English tongue is mightily enriched and gorgeouslie invested in rare ornaments and resplendent abiliments'; Shakespeare is commended for his 'fine filed phrase'. Verse anthologies included more of Shakespeare than of any other writer: not only his poems but also passages from his plays. Verse for the stage was regarded as poetry. Printers passed off the work of others as by Shakespeare in order to increase their sales.

The first substantial comment comes after his death, from fellow actor and writer, Ben Jonson, in the long and carefully considered poem in the 1623 Folio, 'To the memory of my beloved, The AUTHOR / MASTER WILLIAM SHAKESPEARE, AND / what he hath left us': his writings for the stage. 'Soul of the Age!' Jonson calls him: 'The applause, delight, the wonder of our stage!' He prefers him to all other European dramatists, ancient and modern, patriotically declaring:

> Triumph, my Britain, thou hast one to show
> To whom all scenes of Europe homage owe.
> He was not of an age, but for all time!

The elaborate tribute ends with a witty poetical puff, promoting Shakespeare into a constellation: 'Shine forth, thou star of poets!' The constellation would be the Swan, Cygnus: 'Sweet swan of Avon'. The writer of a commendatory poem, the equivalent of a modern publisher's blurb, is not on oath, but the high valuation Jonson expressed in this poem is consistent with the opinion he expressed in his private commonplace book, published after his death as *Discoveries*: 'I loved the man and do honour his memory, on this side idolatry, as much as any. He was, indeed, honest, and of an open and free nature; had an excellent fantasy, brave notions, and gentle expressions, wherein he flowed with that facility that sometime it was necessary he should be stopped.'[2]

Stratford and family

Shakespeare kept his links with Stratford, buying a large house there in 1597, returning there in 1613 and dying in 1616, aged 52. The burial is recorded on 25 April in the register of Holy Trinity of 'Will Shakspeare gent'. *Guglielmus, filius Johannes* of 1564 died Will and a gentleman in 1616. Films about Shakespeare tend to be set in Good Queen Bess's about-to-be-imperial days, and in London, where swashes are buckled and bodices unbuckled, not in the reign of her pacific, unglamorous and intellectually inclined Scottish successor, and not in Stratford. It is notable, however, that Shakespeare rented in London but bought in Stratford, and returned to the banks of the Avon. According to the antiquarian John Aubrey, who 50 years later collected biographical data of this period, Shakespeare had returned home every year. Jonson's poem to his 'beloved' Shakespeare praised him as 'Sweet Swan of Avon', echoing the Greek legend by which the swan is said to sing on its native river before it dies. Homer had been 'the swan of Meander', Virgil 'the swan of Mantua'. Shakespeare went home to Stratford and family. His education, his reading, his life in the theatre and in London enriched his writing, but so did Stratford. We know more about the family and Stratford than we do about Shakespeare in London, and it provides a context worth thinking about. His fresh use of natural detail and his evident knowledge of rural trades and other country activities show Shakespeare not as an urban writer, like Jonson, but always as a countryman.

Shakespeares had lived in Warwickshire for three centuries. William's father, John Shakespeare, had come to Stratford from Snitterfield (four miles north) by 1552. John was a glover, a trade requiring a seven-year apprenticeship. He cured and dyed the skins of sheep, calves and kids – messy physical work, done at home. Everyone's life was then more physical, but Shakespeare hands must have been greasier than most hands in Stratford, and the house in Henley Street not always sweet-smelling. A shepherd says to a court fool: 'Why we are still [constantly] handling our ewes, and their fells, you know, are greasy' (*As You Like It*, 3.2.51–2). John Shakespeare sold his gloves, and traded in wool and other commodities, dealing in property, lending money, and defending his interests in the courts. This craftsman/small businessman married Mary Arden, the daughter of a prosperous local farmer from Wilmcote (four miles north); Mary brought with her 50 acres of land. Ardens had settled in the Forest of Arden, just north of Stratford, five centuries before; they were an established and old-fashioned family. William Shakespeare married Anne Hathaway, the orphan daughter of a yeoman farmer from Shottery (one mile north); almost nothing is known about Anne Shakespeare.[3] He grew up in a small town with woods to the north of the Avon and farms to the south: a fertile country, with orchards, meadows and parks. Life was rural, mercantile, and intensely local.

John Shakespeare's father, Richard, had been a tenant farmer on land in Snitterfield belonging to Mary Arden's father. Mary, the youngest of eight children, was to bear eight children herself. Two daughters died in infancy before William was born, so he was the eldest child as well as the first son. After William came Gilbert, Joan, Anne, Richard and Edmund. Anne died in 1579, aged 8, when William was 15. William's brothers died before him. Joan lived (uninterviewed) until 1646.

John Shakespeare rose in Stratford: he was prominent in its Common Council for 20 years. In 1568, he held its most senior office, that of Bailiff, the equivalent of Mayor, which brought with it the right to a coat of arms. During his year of office, the year in which William turned five, two troupes of professional players acted in the town: Coventry's Play was played nearby on the feast of Corpus Christi, a long day in the summer, the season when companies of players are recorded as passing through Stratford. John features in Council records until 1576, when his long absence from its meetings is noted. In 1592 he is cited as a 'recusant' (from Latin *recusare*, to refuse): one who refused to attend the parish church, as required by law. Some Puritans also refused to go to church, but the word 'recusant' is now used for a Catholic conscientious objector, an abstainer. The Church Commissioners noted that John Shakespeare's absence was 'for fear of process of debt'. The Sheriff's officers could arrest for debt on Sundays, and John's finances seem to have worsened at this time, possibly because of his recusancy.

In 1596 William obtained for his father the grant of the coat of arms to which John's service as Bailiff had entitled him; John owned property worth £500. John signed many surviving documents with his mark – a pair of glover's compasses – or a cross. William's mother Mary Arden signed with her mark, as did his younger daughter Judith. John's office at the Council had required him to look over financial accounts, but he probably could not write. Nick Bottom and his friends, the 'hard-handed' craftsmen of his son's play, *A Midsummer Night's Dream*, are able to read, though Snug the bellows-mender is 'slow of study'.

Catholic England

Born before 1534, John was baptised and brought up a Catholic, as the English had been for nine centuries. Those who accepted the Pope's 1570 excommunication of Elizabeth as illegitimate regarded Mary Queen of Scots as the legitimate Queen of England. Helping Catholic priests to say Mass soon became treason, and there were many executions. Historians now agree that in the 1580s the people of Stratford were still mostly Catholic in sentiment, most of them apparent conformists, 'church papists'. John Shakespeare's 'spiritual will', found in the roof of his house, published in 1790 but later lost, shows that he died a Catholic.

'For fear of process of debt' was an excuse commonly given for recusancy. It could be genuine; it could also be a cover story offered by, or to, Catholics who abstained from Communion. In the 30 years before William Shakespeare's birth, each new reign had seen a new governmental interpretation put on the Communion service, the Eucharist. Henry VIII had defended the Seven Sacraments of the Church against Martin Luther, the chief sacrament being Communion. Henry's book earned him a papal title, 'Defender of the Faith' (the Catholic faith, that is), a title retained by his successors, whether Protestant, Catholic, Anglican or whatever. Henry died in 1547 thinking of himself both as Catholic, a member of the universal church, and also, since 1534, Supreme Governor of its English branch. Under his young son, Edward VI, religion was given a severely Protestant twist; this was sharply reversed as the old form of religion returned to England under Henry's legitimate daughter, Mary Tudor; and again reversed under her half-sister Elizabeth's 'settlement', which removed the teaching that Christ was really present in the Eucharist. Had Mary lived to the age of 69, as her sister Elizabeth did, the future of English Christianity might have been different.

These changes in official religion had a drastic effect on drama: guilds, and their communal civic plays, were suppressed as too Catholic, and religion was entirely forbidden as a subject of drama. They also had general effects. William's parents were cradle Catholics, and John's Catholicism persisted. John was the Council's chief officer when William went to school, but when William left school, his recusant father had not attended Stratford's Common Council for three years. An apparent decline in a father's fortunes (the matter is disputed) would be noticed by an eldest son. John's recusancy may not have been the cause of this apparent decline, and its effects on William remain unknown. Yet if, as is virtually certain, Shakespeare's family and upbringing were strongly pro-Catholic – if he came from a Catholic home – this placed him, initially at least, at a critical distance from the policy of the Elizabethan settlement which created a Church of England. The English Reformation, it is now generally recognised by historians, was largely imposed from above on a perplexed populace. At the time at which Shakespeare left Stratford, many of his contemporaries, perhaps most of them, kept quiet about their religious position.

Education

If John and Mary could not write, their son learned to do so. Stratford school was a medieval grammar school meeting in a single room above the Guildhall (Illustration 4). Its masters held MAs from Oxford University, and some pupils went on to Oxford themselves. Grammar schools schooled their pupils, all boys, in Latin grammar, Latin composition and Latin literature, using modern grammars and rhetorical handbooks written in Latin. Pupils in the upper forms spoke Latin only. A basic drill was double translation, turning passages from Latin into English and English back into Latin, developing grammatical and syntactical dexterity.

Illustration 4 Stratford grammar school. Originally the Guild School, it is above the Guildhall. Shakespeare probably received all his formal education in this room

A schooling so intensely focused on turning and handling words was not wasted on William. Ben Jonson wrote that Shakespeare had 'small [slender] Latin and less Greek'. Neither man attended a university, but the formidable classical learning which the competitive Jonson acquired at Westminster School, and built upon, was one of the few advantages that he had over a senior whom he recognised as his superior.[4] Drummond of Hawthornden tells us that Ben Jonson thought Shakespeare 'wanted art': he was 'incorrect', he should have revised more carefully. As we have seen, this encouraged the later idea of Shakespeare the artless country boy, 'warbling his native woodnotes wild', as the bookish John Milton imagined him. It is misleading to see Shakespeare as a Green Man of English letters, though he obviously had great natural gifts and was free of academic vices. The

son of one of Shakespeare's fellow actors is credibly reported by
John Aubrey to have said that the poet 'understood Latin pretty
well, for he had been in his younger years a school-master in the
country'.[5] A good scholar has judged that 'his plays show he had
received much more than a bare minimum of education; and was
qualified to have taught others what he had himself so intelli-
gently absorbed'.[6] Shakespeare read Euripides in Latin translation
(Greek tragedy in Greek did not reach England till later). He
also read Latin tragedies by Seneca, in Latin or English, and read
Ovid in Latin as well as English. Ovid remained with him for
the rest of his life. 'The witty soul of Ovid lives in mellifluous
and honey-tongued Shakespeare, witness his Venus and Adonis,
his Lucres, his sugared sonnets among his private friends.'[7] The
availability of a range of classics in good texts and in translation
was a relatively new thing, at least in England, due to the labours
of the 'humanists' – men such as Petrarch and Erasmus, More and
Colet, and William Lyly, the Latin grammarian, grandfather of
the accomplished stylist John Lyly. The humanists are so called
as lovers of Latin *litterae humaniores*, 'more humane letters', or
what we call literature. These humanists changed the educational
programme of Europe. (It should be pointed out that Renaissance
humanists, unlike the humanists of the British Humanist
Association, were Christians. They should not be confused, either,
with the 'liberal bourgeois humanists' of Marxist criticism.)

Shakespeare was educated rather than learned, his schooling
intensive rather than advanced. He picked up the rest of his knowledge from conversation, from 30 years spent in the hectic world of
the theatre, from avid reading and from his observation of people
of every kind. But his immersion in the tongue of Rome gave him
an early familiarity with its language that would be the envy of
modern graduates in this subject and of many of their teachers.
It also enabled him to read French, Italian and a little Spanish; he
read widely in those languages as well as in Latin and English. The
ease and dexterity with which Shakespeare manipulates English
were certainly developed by the stiff drilling in Latin he received
at school. He was thoroughly English, and tuned in to all the ways
in which his fellow countrymen actually spoke, but his genius
benefited from a training in the language which informed most
of European literature.

Pupils normally left school at 15, an age William reached in April 1579. At 18, he married a local woman seven or eight years his senior, Anne Hathaway, from nearby Shottery. At the time of the church wedding she was expecting a child, born in 1583 and christened Susanna (it was customary for betrothed couples to consummate their union before the church wedding, though the Church taught otherwise). In 1585 Anne had twins, Hamnet and Judith, probably named after Hamnet and Judith Sadler, thought to be their godparents.[8]

We do not know how the 20-year-old father of three supported his family. In 1681 John Aubrey consulted Christopher Beeston, the son of one of Shakespeare's fellow actors. Beeston is the source of the report that Shakespeare 'understood Latin pretty well' and that he 'had been in his younger years a school-master in the country'. When we next hear of him, however, he is in London. Robert Greene's coded attack of 1592 suggests that the 'puppet' borrowed lines from his betters, and that his plays stole their thunder. After 1595, his work shows improvement. Single plays began to appear in Quarto editions. He was one of the original partners in the leading company of actors, the Lord Chamberlain's Men, founded in 1594, which played in the Theatre, rebuilt in 1599 as the Globe. As a 'sharer', Shakespeare took his share of the company's profits. He was the only playwright who was a sharer, and the only playwright who wrote exclusively for one company. In 1603 the new King, more interested in plays than the old Queen, made this company the King's Men. They played at Court as well as at the Globe and, from 1609, at the indoor Blackfriars theatre, especially in winter.

The main family events of Shakespeare's later life can baldly be summarised as follows. In 1596 his son Hamnet died, aged 11. Next year, William bought the largest private house in Stratford, New Place. In 1601 his father died. In 1607, his daughter Susanna married John Hall, a noted physician. In the next year Susanna bore a daughter, Elizabeth, the only grandchild William would see, and in the following year his mother died. From 1611 he spent more time in Stratford. In February 1616 his daughter Judith married, and on 23 April 1616, William died. Judith's first child, called Shakespeare, was born and died later that year. William Shakespeare was buried in the chancel of Holy Trinity, Stratford, where, some time before 1623, his monument was erected.

3

Plays

If we turn now from Shakespeare's life to the obscure beginnings of his work, it is reasonable to suppose that he must have been in London by 1588, writing collaboratively but prominently the plays whose success so irritated Robert Greene. We cannot exactly date the composition of his first plays: four histories, three comedies and a tragedy. Classical drama was then available in Latin only, but 'tragedy' and 'comedy' are Greek terms for Greek forms of drama, saluting the Athenian drama of two thousand years earlier.

The first substantial public theatre in Britain since Roman times was built in 1576. Its name, the Theatre, invoked classic precedent. The builder was James Burbage, a joiner or carpenter. His wooden Theatre stood in Shoreditch, north of the walls and outside the regulatory powers of the City of London. Its timbers were taken down in 1599 by the Chamberlain's Men and re-erected as the Globe, a new playhouse on Bankside, south of the City and of the river Thames. Burbage would have been surprised to learn that the plays put on in his Theatre would one day be rated more highly than the works of Sir Philip Sidney and Edmund Spenser. Sir Thomas Bodley, who refounded the library of Oxford University, which had been stripped under Edward VI, at about the time of the composition of *Hamlet*, told his librarian not to collect worthless plays, classing them as 'idle bookes, & riffe raffes'.[1] Bodley, a Calvinist, had been educated in Geneva.

In 1579 Sir Philip Sidney, in response to a Puritan attack on the stage, wrote *An Apology for Poetry*, a general defence of imaginative literature. Sidney regarded contemporary English plays as 'neither right tragedies, nor right comedies'. According to the model which Italian Renaissance theorists had extracted from Aristotle and erected into rules, genre should be pure: tragedy grave and noble, comedy low and ridiculous; no laughs in tragedy, no tears in comedy. The wonderful Sidney died in battle in 1586, aged 32; had he lived to 64, he could have seen all Shakespeare's plays, and might have overlooked their offences against 'right' genre. But such objections to Shakespeare's 'mixed' drama, and to his breaches of the classical Unities, persisted until Dr Johnson demolished them.[2]

Strictly speaking, Shakespeare did not 'mix' tragedy and comedy, since there were no such categories in the plays of the native tradition. Pre-Elizabethan drama is ignored by many writers on Shakespeare, but he and his contemporaries grew up with expectations derived from a European tradition four centuries old in England. Medieval drama, which began with the Passiontide and Easter plays that are still performed in some Catholic countries, had moved out of the church and into the street a century before Chaucer, who died in 1400. The guild or mystery plays, dramatising biblical stories in day-long cycles on summer holy days, were still played in Shakespeare's youth at a series of processional stages in the streets of cities such as York, Wakefield, Chester and Coventry. It was once taught that the mystery plays had naturally faded away, being medieval and Catholic, and that this was followed by the Renaissance, a fruit of which was a modern drama which naturally chose to be secular. In fact, the day-long cycles of religious plays performed by city guilds were still being performed when the Theatre was built in London. A cycle was performed at Coventry on the feast of the Body of Christ, Corpus Christi, 29 June 1579. As Coventry is only 19 miles from Stratford, Shakespeare, then aged 15 and probably a school leaver, could conceivably have been seen this cycle, which ends with Christ's passion, death and resurrection. He would certainly have been aware of this tradition of plays and of playing.[3]

All such plays, like other forms of communal religion, were suppressed by decrees of Elizabeth's government around 1580 (though one Coventry guild kept its pageant wagon until the 1630s). The government then forbade religion to appear on the stage; it was too hot a topic, and the stage tradition was both Catholic and popular. The Corpus Christi plays had no unity of place or time: they dramatised the whole story of creation in one long June day. In these open-air popular enactments of the bible story, each episode was put on by the workers of a different guild, though the carpenters' guild had a more general involvement since they built the stages. The Theatre itself was built by a carpenter, James Burbage, and its rebuilt timbers built the Globe. Shakespeare's father was an artisan, and popular craft traditions underpin Shakespeare's artfulness.

Carpenters were especially responsible for the play of Noah: they could build an Ark. Scripture gained in humour: Noah's wife doesn't believe in her husband's theory of the Flood and refuses to go into the Ark, threatening to ruin the story, like the legendary innkeeper in the primary school nativity play who opens his door to say that there is plenty of room in the inn. One of the shepherds in a northern nativity play is Mac, a sheep-stealer; a stolen lamb is substituted for the Christ child. Medieval popular immersion in religion was such that seriousness could switch to jocularity and back again. In a Cain and Abel play, God is greeted by Cain's question to Abel: 'Who is that hob over the wall?' (A hob is a clown, an oaf.) The actor who played God was paid one penny. Noah's Ark is built on the stage, Eve and Mary talk to each other, time and place do not matter: ultimate reality is metaphysical. Such playing, both sacred and popular, was neither tragic nor comic but both almost at once. The sacred is not treated with consistent respect; there is no decorum. This appearance of jumbled tragicomedy is what the enlightened in the eighteenth century called 'Gothic' – rightly, since 'Gothic' was the term for all things medieval; the word 'medieval' did not come into English until 1817. The incongruity in Shakespeare's plays, notably the appearance of clowns and fools in tragedy, is not classical but medieval, Gothic, indecorous. The carved decoration of Gothic churches is frequently indecorous. These biblical plays full of popular humour were written by clerics for performance by citizens.

Puritans among English Reformers wished to rid religion of visual or physical images, so that all would worship one God, not through the sacred drama of the Mass, not through ceremonies, but only through words, with no intermediaries other than the words of Scripture. The Reformers suppressed civic drama, and the Tudor monarchy eventually appropriated to itself the processions and pageantry of popular religion. The cult of Elizabeth the Virgin Queen notoriously borrowed from that of the Mother of Christ. Some of the pull of the old civic drama also passed to the words and actions performed in the new permanent public theatres, as drama once again proved highly popular with all classes.

The old Morality plays, later than the mystery plays, gave a large part to the Vice, a wicked but entertaining figure who is finally defeated and dismissed. Marlowe stuffed the middle of his *Dr Faustus* with this kind of farce. Shakespeare's Falstaff is a developed version of the Vice figure. But Shakespeare's debt to the unclassified tradition of English plays is general, not specific. Unexpectedness is part of this tradition, which, as Dr Johnson pointed out in his dismissal of the Unities, reflects the actuality of a world 'in which at the same time the reveller is hasting to his wine, and the mourner burying his friend'.[4] Shakespeare puts on stage the gatekeeper of the Macbeths' castle, who, as he drunkenly responds to a knocking at the gate, imagines that he is the 'porter of hell-gate' – fittingly enough, as his master has just murdered a sleeping guest, his lord. A more extended example begins with the gravediggers in *Hamlet*: comic banter switches to Hamlet's 'Alas, poor Yorick', when a disinterred skull turns out to be that of a favourite jester who had played with Hamlet when he was a child. The Prince's sadness then turns to horror when he learns that the grave is being dug for Ophelia, whom he had loved. There is more to say of the clowning in Shakespearian tragedy, but all his plays, before they are comedies or tragedies, are plays – an English word without the generic apartheid of the Greek terms.

4
Shake-scene

First plays

1589–92	*The Taming of the Shrew*
1590–1	*The Two Gentlemen of Verona*
1591	*2 Henry VI*
1591	*3 Henry VI*
1591–2	*Titus Andronicus*
1592	*1 Henry VI*
1592–4	*Richard III*
1594	*The Comedy of Errors*

(Dates of composition are conjectural.)

What kind of scene?

What kind of scene did Shakespeare shake? Permanent theatres were a new thing, and their repertoire was also new. It was no longer civic and communal, as medieval drama had been; and its former religious subject matter was now forbidden to it by law. It was not academic, like the translated classical plays appreciated by university audiences. It was no longer dependent on the decision of the owner of a great house or of a coaching inn. The actors belonged to the companies (initially travelling companies) which had replaced the civic guilds. Each company had a noble patron: Leicester's Players, Strange's Men, the Lord Chamberlain's Men. Although the companies had noble patrons and could play at court, they were commercial enterprises like joint-stock companies and their performances were typically public, though they also performed in private. In London inn-yards of the 1550s, the spectator had put his penny in a box at the entrance (hence 'box-office'). In 1576 came James Burbage's polygonal Theatre, an amphitheatre open to the sky, built for the Earl of Leicester's players but public and permanent. There was a new appetite for drama, a craze which explored the interests of a large new audience. The Theatre, built north of the City walls, was the home of diversions not permitted in the City (Illustration 5).

In 1599 the Theatre was re-erected as the Globe on the south bank of the Thames. It stood three storeys high, a polygon of 22 sides, close to Southwark Cathedral, surrounded by other churches, houses and shops, but also by 'tippling houses', theatres, brothels, cockpits and bear pits. Puritans mistrusted the theatre, but the Court watched it and licensed it; and a play could not be put on without a licence from the Lord Chamberlain. The Globe could hold almost 3000 – more than the population of Stratford-upon-Avon. (When the rebuilt Globe was opened in 1996, it was found to have good acoustics and a surprisingly intimate feel.) There were then five other big theatres in London serving a population of under 200,000 people.

Ten days counted as a long run, and revivals were not the rule. New plays were always needed. Rehearsals could not be lengthy, and there were no spare copies of the complete script, so each player had no more than his written 'part', with cues and speeches. The plays were put on at 2 p.m. in this enclosed yard with its roofed stage and thatched galleries; the apron stage pushed out into the middle of the auditorium. Shakespeare mentions 'the two hours' traffic of the stage'; no time spent shifting scenery. All depended on the players, their rich costumes and simple props, and the words supplied by the player from Stratford. The action flowed: as one scene ended, another would begin. A player entered saying, 'This castle has a pleasant seat' or 'Is this a dagger that I see before me?', so that the audience would know what to imagine. The audience did not suspend disbelief within a darkened theatre: it collaborated in daylit make-believe. Shakespeare often tells the audience, through the players, exactly what to imagine: 'But look the morn in russet mantle clad / Walks o'er the dew of yon high

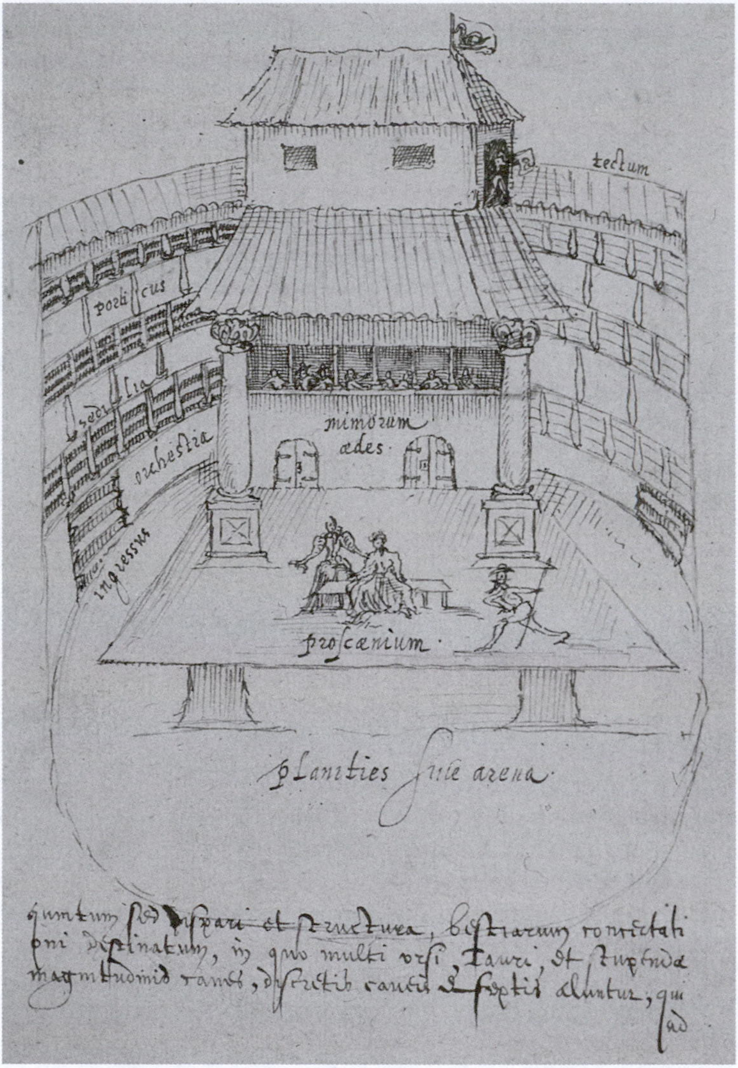

Illustration 5 Aernout van Buchel's copy of the drawing of the Swan play-house, made by his friend Johannes de Witt while visiting London in *c.*1596

Key: *tectum* roof; *porticus* gallery; *sedilia* seats; *ingressus* entry; *mimorum aedes* the actors' house; *proscaenium* fore-stage; *planities sive arena* flat space or arena.

eastward hill' (*Hamlet*, 1.1.171–2), or 'Sit, Jessica. Look how the floor of heaven / Is thick inlaid with patens of bright gold' (*The Merchant of Venice*, 5.1.58–9).

Most theatres today try to create an illusion of reality, but visual illusion at the Globe was largely a matter of costume. The sexually experienced Cleopatra was played by a boy, as were all women's parts. Verse is itself a convention, as are stage dialogue, 'aside' and soliloquy. So is invisibility. In broad daylight an actor would whisper 'I am invisible'; he was not invisible to those whom Shakespeare calls the groundlings, and Jonson 'the understanding gentlemen of the ground', standing at his feet in the pit: visible, audible and inhalable, crowding round the stage.[1] Those who paid one penny to stand cannot have heard or grasped every flying word or exactly followed Shakespeare's rapidly evolving sentences. But learning then was normally done through the ear, not the eye, and there was an appetite for patterned language; crowds flocked to hear John Donne's two-hour sermons as they did to animal-baiting pits. Theatre was popular; the Globe could hold a sizeable fraction of those Londoners who were free to attend. Drama had the draw of a sporting event; the audience participated, as at an opera in a small town in Italy, a Spanish bull-fight, a British pantomime or a big game in the United States. The cultural mix meant that popular vigour and crudity rubbed shoulders with poetry and intelligence.

Shakespeare came in on a rising tide, which, for him, led on to fortune. Public drama was crude and refined, sensational and complex; private theatres were indoor, smaller, quieter and more expensive to attend. But public theatres drew from all sections of society physically able to attend: high and low, coarse and fine, simple and sophisticated. English Renaissance drama had rhetorical eloquence and the intellectual input and structure given by the Christian humanist education of the grammar schools and universities. But it was the popular draw which gave the medium its cultural power, without which its enactment of current and recurrent human issues might have lacked vigour, salt, variety, humour, impact. The focus of some academic critics on this writer's intelligence and subtlety is justified, but it must not be forgotten that he learned his trade and plied it in the popular theatre, playing to the eye as well as the ear, and to the cultural instinct as well as to the intellect.

Immediate predecessors

In his poem to the memory of Shakespeare, Jonson wrote, 'how farre thou didst our Lily out-shine, / Or sporting Kid, or Marlowe's mighty line'. Of Shakespeare's lesser predecessors, Lyly is 'polite' (polished to a shine), but other University Wits, Robert Greene, Thomas Lodge and Thomas Nashe, wrote both for court patrons and new urban patrons of less elegant tastes. They wrote prose romances, unlike Shakespeare, who later drew on Lodge's *Rosalynde* for *As You Like It*, and, very much later on, Robert Greene's *Pandosto* for *The Winter's Tale*. Shakespeare, the 'puppet' of Greene's attack, wrote scripts for his own company, saving it money and removing the chance of a commission from other writers. As a 'sharer', he made a considerable amount of money from his partnership, though less than Richard Burbage, the company's leading actor, or the fortune made by Edward Alleyn, the leading actor of a rival company. More money could be made in the theatre than printed books could ever make. There were many playwrights, and Shakespeare collaborated a good deal both at the beginning and the end of his career.[2]

Of Shakespeare's talented immediate predecessors, Thomas Kyd (1558–94) was long remembered for *The Spanish Tragedy*, later subtitled *Hieronymo is Mad Again*, the archetype of the brilliantly plotted revenge play. He may also have written a lost play about Hamlet. Shakespeare learned suspense, surprise and construction from Kyd. He had a more literary debt to the poems and plays of the precocious Christopher Marlowe, born in the same year as himself, 1564. Jonson praised the mightiness Marlowe gave his 'line', the blank or unrhymed pentameter. Marlowe's iambic verse has the regularity of a military march, and his speeches ask to be declaimed with energy. His themes were appetite, pride and ambition – and their outcomes. His first hit, *Tamburlaine the Great*, staged in 1587, was a two-part pageant in which the shepherd Tamburlaine conquers Asia, crushing enemy after enemy in a repeating pattern. His hubris in challenging the gods is not punished; he merely dies. Like the protagonists of Marlowe's *The Jew of Malta* and *Dr Faustus*, Tamburlaine is an upstart who scorns human limits. Dr Faustus, an intellectual sceptic, was often misread by nineteenth-century liberals as a rebel defying old authority, whose aspirations were like those of Goethe's Faust. This overlooks the middle of the play, in which Faustus sells his soul for 24 years of cheap fun, paltry knowledge and schoolboy stunts. The beginning and end of *Faustus* are brilliant, but the rest is stuffed with the crude jests of the Vice of the old morality plays, and with devils who finally claim the unrepentant sinner. Some lines from the final moral will have echoed after their author's own violent departure from life:

> Cut is the branch that might have grown full straight,
> And burned is Apollo's laurel bough,
> That sometime grew within this learned man.
> Faustus is gone! Regard his hellish fall ...

This forceful power of language was new to the English stage. Faustus had earlier, in Act 5, Scene 1, conjured up an image of Helen of Troy:

> 'Is this the face that launched a thousand ships
> And burnt the topless towers of Ilium?
> Sweet Helen, make me immortal with a kiss:
> Her lips suck forth my soul, see where it flies.'

Aspiration transmutes into the delusive glamour of sexual desire: 'O thou art fairer than the evening air, / Clad in the beauty of a thousand stars.' Marlowe gives Christian lines the same rhetorical projection: 'See, see, where Christ's blood streams in the firmament!' cries the despairing Faustus. Sin and hell are sensational, and good for the box-office. For all the power of Marlowe's verse, however, the extinguishing of such aspirations seems not providential justice but sardonic, even gleeful.

The protagonist of *The Jew of Malta* is called after the murderer in the Gospel narratives of the Passion, Barabas. A cunning trickster, he gleefully blows up a convent of nuns, including his daughter, a convert to Christianity, and falls into a cauldron of boiling oil he had prepared for his guests. The Catholic defenders and Turkish attackers of Malta are shown as being as amoral as Barabas, but lack his cynical zest. Like Faustus, Barabas drops into hell, a blackly comic exposé of hypocrisy. The Prologue, spoken by Machiavel, is gleefully impious: 'I count religion but a childish toy, / And hold there is no sin but ignorance.' Machiavel also says: 'Admired I am by those who hate me most'; 'admired' means 'wondered at', but suggests the fascination of Marlowe. The final screams of Barabas show that, like Faustus, he disbelieved in the reality of what awaited him.

Screams also end Marlowe's *Edward II*, one of the earliest history plays, and a workmanlike study in the operation of power: the weak king loses his throne to nobles who resent his homosexual infatuation with the low-born Gaveston and conspire with his wife to depose him. The killing of Edward gave Shakespeare a pattern of pathos for his *Richard II*, and his *Merchant of Venice* revises Marlowe's *Jew*. Marlowe's play construction can be feeble and his characters flat; Shakespeare's kind of humanism has its own scepticism but has Christian roots, whereas Marlowe seems to be materialist with some added Christian morality. Marlowe's seven plays lack the tragic complexity of late Shakespeare, but Marlowe was killed at 28, and no later writer of tragedy in English comes near to Shakespeare. Marlowe is disturbing, sensationalist, lurid; but his verse is as eloquent as Shakespeare's and has its own fierce brilliance.

First plays

Two of the plays listed at the head of this chapter, *The Taming of the Shrew* and *The Comedy of Errors*, are true comedies, ending in marriage and reunion. They go well on the stage, ingeniously developing a situation strong in human interest. Shakespeare constructs and unfolds the action with skill, but the basic situation is simple, as is the humour (too simple for some modern tastes), though the climax of each play is complex. *The Taming of the Shrew* is an 'ordeal' story from folk tale, and *The Comedy of Errors* is directly based on a Latin play by Plautus (*c*.254–184 BC) about the identical Antipholus twins. (Shakespeare, who knew this play from schooldays, was the father of twins, a boy and a girl.) The apprentice playwright was confident enough to give the Antipholus twins identical twin servants both named Dromio, and to manage the complications. Doubling and alternation were to become two of his favourite devices. The last scene of *The Shrew*, in which Kate, the virago 'tamed' by Petruchio, finally obeys her husband so that he – or they, for they are two of a kind – will win a bet, is a theatrical coup, leaving modern audiences and readers to wonder about the sincerity of her obedience. But the sincerity of a staged public act is always open to interpretation, and drama is an especially open form of representation.

Titus Andronicus, like *The Comedy of Errors*, has Latin sources. It is a political tragedy from early Roman history, featuring 27 on-stage deaths, some of which occur halfway through a rhyming couplet. A messenger enters holding two heads and a hand; Lavinia, raped twice off-stage, has her hands and tongue cut off, but tells us on-stage who did this by writing in the sand with a 'staff' held in her mouth. Elizabethan spectators did not faint at classical atrocity. Their theatres were built like animal-baiting pits; a bear pit, Paris Garden, stood near the Globe, and Hollar's *Long View* confused the two buildings (Illustration 6). The Prologue to *Henry V* compares the theatre to a cock-fighting arena: 'Can this cockpit hold the vasty fields of France?' Londoners could also see Catholic priests 'hung, drawn and quartered' at Tyburn and Smithfield; their heads were displayed on London Bridge, near the Globe ('drawn': a skilful executioner drew out the heart to show it to the dying man). When Hamlet says to Rosencrantz and Guildenstern, set to spy on him, 'You would pluck out the heart of my mystery' (3.2.355–6), he speaks metaphorically but he thinks as some Catholics thought.

Titus, a 'tragedy of blood', is partly modelled on the tragedies of Seneca. Seneca was tutor, then minister, to Nero, a Roman emperor mentioned in *Hamlet* and in *King Lear*, and had to execute Nero's atrocious whims – such as feeding Christians to lions. Seneca's plays are appropriately *noir*. When Nero turned against his minister in AD 69, the Stoic Seneca summoned his friends and staged a philosopher's suicide modelled on that of Socrates. Seneca believed in the Stoic philosophy of rational restraint; his plays sensationalise the evil results of unrestrained passion. Though Shakespeare could read Seneca in Latin, ten of his plays had been translated into English by the Jesuit Jasper Heywood, and published in 1581. The educated men who read such plays might have thought about the Senecan fates of Wolsey, More and Cromwell, successive ministers of Henry VIII. The Jesuit Edmund Campion suffered martyrdom in that year. It is generally believed that Seneca wrote to be read privately in the 'closet' or

Illustration 6 Detail of Wenceslaus Hollar's engraving, *Long View of London* (1641), looking north and west across the Thames. The drawing, done with optical instruments, is very accurate, but what Hollar labels 'The Globe', its flag showing above the river, was a bear pit. The 'Beer-bayting house', to the left and further from the bank, is the Globe Theatre as rebuilt in 1613

study, not performed on the stage; but the unsqueamish English saw the blood that the Romans only read about and imagined. English Seneca was *rouge* as well as *noir*.

There are three English histories (a new form perfected by Shakespeare), dramatising narratives found in the popular prose chronicles of Hall and Holinshed, which recounted the events of reigns previous to that of Henry Tudor in 1485. (Raphael Holinshed was the leading compiler of a compendium of the *Chronicles of England, Scotland, and Ireland*, published in 1577, enlarged in 1587. The chief source of all Shakespeare's history plays, it was also a source of *Macbeth*, *King Lear*, and *Cymbeline*.) Whereas tragedy ends in death, and comedy in marriage, chronicle retails a tangle of events, and these events have to be selected from, put in order and recreated into dialogues and scenes. The three *Henry VI* plays are loosely constructed, pageant-like epic drama, patriotic, military and spectacular, though they treat the fall of favourites as tragic.[3] Unlike these dramatised chronicles, *Richard III* is a drama, effective on stage. The Quarto title was *The Tragedy of Richard of York*, and it conforms to a medieval idea of tragedy: the fall of a man of great estate. The action is based on Holinshed and on Thomas More's prose *History of Richard III* (1513), a study in tyranny. Shakespeare gave its events a Senecan character, but developed his twisted plotter from More's account. Compared with medieval chroniclers, who saw events in terms of personal agency and divine Providence, humanists like More wrote analytic history in the mode of the Roman historian Tacitus. Richard III, who is also modelled on the Vice figure from the morality plays, is not simply either mischievous or a malignant. He is the first of Shakespeare's protagonists to soliloquise, a development first found in the morality play *Everyman* of 1495, which has a central figure whose soliloquies show internal consciousness. *Richard III* is an early example of Shakespeare's ability to synthesise literary and theatrical traditions of quite different kinds.

The writing in what may be his earliest surviving play, *The Two Gentlemen of Verona*, is already accomplished. It is a love comedy, with ingredients which recur in several later romance comedies: an Italian romance setting, a duke, young rivals, a father called Antonio, a daughter who dresses as a boy to follow her lover, a ring, a glove, a friar's cell, comic servants, and a song – 'Who is

Silvia?' Romances were stories of marvellous adventure, often ending in the reunion of young lovers or of divided families, or both.
Shakespeare's kind of romance was comedic rather than comic:
not harshly satiric nor full of farcical incidents, as contemporary
comedies typically were, but with a happy ending. Comedy was
easier to write than history, as a history play had to convert chronicle events into drama. In comedy there were established models
to hand in Roman comedy and in medieval romance, and in the
stylish verbal wit made fashionable by John Lyly. Comedy also had
a box of ready-made theatrical tricks, including disguise (never
penetrated), mistaken identity (never confessed or discovered
before Act 5), and the different views of love taken by masters and
servants, parents and children, men and women. Such a comedic
alternation of perspective, creating contrast and variety, became a
structural principle in nearly all Shakespeare's plays.

Having considered the theatre Shakespeare worked in, his
immediate predecessors and the plays of his apprenticeship, we
should look now at the media he worked in: language and verse.

Language

The theatre Shakespeare wrote for was bare of scenery, a 'wooden
O' open to the sky. Language therefore had far more to do than
it does in a modern proscenium arch theatre, in which, after the
curtain goes up, a darkened audience sees a well-lit simulation of
visual reality: a kind of illusion closer to cinema than to open-air
performance. What was then the state of the English language?
Francis Meres wrote that by Shakespeare 'the English tongue is
mightily enriched and gorgeouslie invested in rare ornaments and
resplendent abiliments'.[4] The aspiration of Renaissance humanists throughout Europe was that their vernaculars would develop
a literature like that of Latin. In Italy, Tuscan had gone far towards
doing so. But they feared that these local vernaculars would not
last. Latin was such that its literature had been read for nearly 2000
years. English, by contrast, had changed alarmingly since Chaucer's
death in 1400, as was already remarked on during the reign of Henry
VIII. It is luckily the case that Shakespeare, like the King James Bible,
remains largely intelligible without special study. The structure of
English has probably changed less since 1616 than it did between

Chaucer and Shakespeare. But English humanists, admiring Virgil and Cicero, noted the instability of their own tongue and doubted its adequacy and dignity. Francis Meres had the preference of the conventionally sophisticated for gorgeous imports; others, however, objected to 'inkhorn' terms copied out of foreign books, adulterating the native Saxon plainness. The language experts we hear from most often today rejoice in language change, but Renaissance humanists, whose concern was literature, worried about the future of their unstable vernacular. Might the influx from Latin, Greek, Italian and French devalue English? It did not, and Shakespeare benefited from this top-dressing of the language.

English had not been unmixedly Saxon even in 1066; after that time it increasingly became a cross between Old English and French, the language of Norman government. When written English regained parity with French in the 1360s, it resurfaced in a Frenchified form and in a wild variety of dialects. The first king who preferred to speak English rather than French was Henry V (d.1422). In the time between Chaucer and Shakespeare, dialectal difference had reduced in the written form of the language, and London's written standard spread outside London. But written English changed a great deal in the fifteenth century: vowels shifted, stresses moved, endings simplified, grammar and syntax altered. Readers who have never seen Elizabethan spelling or Shakespeare's handwriting are in for a shock. More than 80 spellings of the name 'Shakespeare' are found, and Shakespeare (see Illustration 3, p. 14) spelled his own name differently in each of his six surviving signatures. Structural fundamentals less obvious than spelling remained unsettled in a language as yet little affected by the standardising effect of print. English was molten, not set. This is one reason why late-medieval English and Elizabethan English both seem fresher in their idiom than that of later periods – more free, flexible and exuberant. The English of the reigns of Henry VII and Henry VIII, in comparison with that of Chaucer and of Shakespeare, seems plainer and stiffer.

Extravagance was enjoyed, in language and in the performance of public life. The Elizabethan ruling class liked the prodigious – witness Sir Walter Raleigh's colonial schemes, the 'prodigy houses' of great families, and the ambitious scale of such works as Philip Sidney's *Arcadia* (230,000 words) and Edmund Spenser's less-than-half-finished *The Faerie Queene* (33,000 lines). Elizabethan

Golden Age expansiveness peaked with the Armada of 1588, before a Shakespeare play had reached the stage. If his talent was expansive, his early histories show no optimism about politics. A change towards scepticism, satire and succinctness became general in the 1590s, but is seen in Francis Bacon, Ben Jonson and John Donne sooner than in Shakespeare. His narrative poems are full of elaborately eloquent speeches, though it should again be noted that the eloquence proves ineffectual.

In his plays Shakespeare's quick grasp and verbal facility can run ahead of understanding. Shakespeare's audience were close to him in the cockpit of the Globe. But no audience, even in the hush of a modern auditorium, can ever have caught every trick of Shakespeare's verbal comedy or each turn of thought in a tragic soliloquy. Even a prose conversation designed to impart initial information can cause a scholarly reader to blink. *King Lear* begins with two earls discussing Lear's planned division of the kingdom. Gloucester responds to Kent's opening enquiry with a speech that ends: '[e]qualities are so weighed that curiosity in neither can make choice of either's moiety'. The curlicues of courtly talk are what might be expected between earls in a tragedy. But did the audience understand Gloucester's point, that the division of the kingdom has been so nicely calculated that no portion is more desirable than another? Complication is what Shakespeare often brings to the stories he takes from his sources, as well as to language. But the 'two hours traffic of the stage' imposed some economy. The disciplined Ben Jonson thought that his friend's fancy and facility needed more control. Jonson makes himself clearer than Shakespeare, but, except in his more fantastic comic writing, the tightness of his rein is almost visible, whereas Shakespeare seems at ease. His challenge was to keep his linguistic facility in balance with his openness to mental complexity, a challenge which became more pressing in his later plays as his thinking accelerated and he became less patient in fully working out its expression.[5]

Verse

The normal medium of Shakespeare's plays is verse. Verse had for centuries been the usual medium of popular literature, both stories in ballad form and the longer narratives of romances and of plays.

Verse is easier than prose to remember and to recite, a winning consideration for performers who were not always very literate. The advent of printing is one of the Good Things of history; without it we would probably not have Shakespeare's plays. But technical advances bring loss as well as gain. Language composed for performance, whether from altars, pulpits or stages, is more rhythmical than language written for silent reading. Print is partly to blame for the auditory inferiority of modern plays to those of Shakespeare's generation, and the inferiority of modern Bible translations to the English of the King James Bible. The volume of material in print has long been so great that we normally read quickly and silently, whereas verse and drama should be read aloud, or sounded in the head. Rapid silent reading ignores rhythm and weakens memory.

Verse has lost its historic public role in England. Until after the First World War, verse on public subjects could be read in national newspapers, but it is scarcely an exaggeration to say that today verse (outside the classroom) is chiefly found in little magazines devoted to poetry and little else; in the obituary column of the local newspaper; and in the work of Shakespeare. Poems are usually short, often personal, even private. Poetry can at moments of celebration or loss be recalled to public service, and the verse of the past lives on, in books and in the memories of some. In contemporary literature, however, the medium of verse has been sidelined. Some students of literature at university actively avoid poetry courses, a reflection on their schooling. An introductory book about reading Shakespeare in the twenty-first century must address the subject of verse directly – verse, not poetry. This may seem a digression, and the eyes of weaker students of English glaze over when discussion becomes even slightly technical. But verse is not an irrelevance. On the contrary, since Shakespeare was a verse dramatist, the question is unavoidable. It should in any case be of interest to a student of literature and to anyone who attends a Shakespeare play.

Verse, metrical composition, was in Shakespeare's day the usual medium of drama and of much else. Poetry, in contrast, is a qualitative term, and 'poetry' may nowadays seem precious. Moreover, the word 'poetry' may create an expectation of personal self-expression which is alien to drama. Shakespeare wrote mostly in lines of 'blank' (that is, unrhymed) verse, a form which nineteenth-century students of classical metre labelled 'iambic pentameter'. A pentameter has five metres, or measures, or 'feet'. Greek verse used a combination of musical pitch and syllabic length or quantity; a syllable was short or long (two shorts equalled one long). An iamb or iambic foot had a short syllable followed by a long one. The Greek system was adopted by Latin poets, and at the Renaissance was transferred to English.

But English is a stressed, not a quantitative, language, and its verse is therefore based on stresses, not on syllabic length. An 'iambic' foot in English verse has an unstressed syllable followed by a stressed syllable. Iambic pentameter has ten syllables with a regularly alternating beat, beginning with an off-beat:

> 'Is *this* the *face* that *launched* a *thous*and *ships*?'

This was the line which Marlowe made 'mighty'. It regularises an 'unstress–stress' pattern, common in spoken English, and is one of the least artificial kinds of verse (although 'artificial' in 1590 was a word of praise, not of censure). 'Stress–unstress', the reverse of the iamb, is a trochee. Trochaic verse produces a very different effect. Here is how Puck begins the epilogue to *A Midsummer Night's Dream*, in trochaic tetrameter (and rhyme):

> *If* we *shad*ows *have* of*fend*ed,
> *Think* but *this*, and *all* is *mend*ed:
> *That* you *have* but *slumb*'red *here*,
> *While* these *vis*ions *did* ap*pear*.
> (5.1.425–9)

This example also shows that a four-foot line has a rocking-horse quality, whereas the five-foot line, with no opportunity for a mid-line pause, maintains a steadier movement.

In his earlier plays Shakespeare, like Marlowe, maintains a regular coincidence of speech-stress and verse-stress, a foundational achievement. He also made the pause at the end of the iambic verse line regularly coincide with a break in the sense. Such 'end-stopped' lines were readily memorised by players and recognised as verse units by hearers. A series of end-stopped iambic pentameters creates a regular cadence and an expectation of regularity. Once audiences had got used to this, Shakespeare could allow speech-stress and metrical stress to diverge, as they do in the verse of his later plays, where the beat becomes unpredictable; likewise the sense runs over the end of the verse line, as in these lines from the middle of a speech by Florizel to Perdita in *The Winter's Tale*:

> ... when you do dance, I wish you
> A wave o' th' sea, that you might ever do
> Nothing but that, move still, still so,
> And own no other function.
>
> (4.4.140–3)

Shakespeare made less and less use of rhyme in his plays, though he put songs and sonnets into his comedies and songs into some histories and tragedies – except in the classical plays (though a song is memorably placed in *Julius Caesar*). A moral rhyming couplet is often used to mark the end of a scene. Thus Hamlet clinches Act 2 with 'The play's the thing / Wherein I'll catch the conscience of the king.' Shakespeare also used prose, formal and informal, chiefly in comedy. His best prose – the prose of Bottom, Falstaff or Shylock – is as good as his best verse. The same cannot be said of his poet predecessors. Geoffrey Chaucer's verse can walk or run or dance, but his prose stumbles.

In the theory of rhetoric then prevailing, high style should be used for the fall of kings and low style for the ridiculous follies of mankind. Tragedy should be in verse, and comedy in prose. Shakespeare's early plays, however, are all in verse, except for comic scenes between servants; his *Richard II* (1595–6) was the last non-comic play to have no prose. The contrast between verse and prose was then very marked, especially, as it seems, in the rather formal manner in which verse was delivered from the stage. The contrast was almost as marked as that between aria and recitative in oratorio or opera. This either/or contrast, when combined with a graduated register of styles, a hierarchy from high to low, allows the dramatist to range from regular verse in grand language to irregular verse in common speech, or vice versa, and also from formal prose to casual backchat. It also provided great auditory variety. Speech is the chief means by which Shakespeare could give detailed reality to character. This sense of reality is, however, conveyed through speech conventions very unlike those of real life. The conveyance of meaning and feeling is the primary function of language, but is not its only effect, for speech has its pattern and its rhythms. Sense is conveyed by a train of sounds that follow the traffic rules for language, the rules of grammar and syntax. Even the most informal speech follows a grammatical order which has its own rules and patterning.

Spoken verse adds to these patterns a set of musical rhythms, so that the pattern of sense plays against the patterns of sound. The heightened rhythm of verse, either spoken by the human voice or mentally articulated and heard in the inner ear, has physiological and emotional effects, as readers of such lines as these might agree:

> When to the sessions of sweet silent thought
> I summon up remembrance of things past ...
>
> (Sonnet 30, 1–2)

Modern definitions of poetry usually focus on words and meaning: 'the right words in the right order'; 'these words in these positions'; 'language charged with meaning to the greatest possible degree'. But language is far more than an informational code. In the lines quoted above, sounds give shape to sense, and verse, at its best, lends these shapes a harmony which amplifies the sense and endears it to the ear. Verse is fundamental to poetry, since its metre and rhythm affect listeners more deeply than in the looser harmony of prose. Such affects, instinctual not intellectual, help to make speech memorable. Another modern definition of poetry, 'memorable speech', describes exactly what Shakespeare, as player-poet-scriptwriter, had to provide for his fellow players, his hearers and his readers. Shakespeare thought in terms of words to be spoken. We should not have these words had they not been printed in Quarto or Folio, but it is best to read them aloud.

5
Dramatist

Second set of plays

1595	*Love's Labour's Lost*
1595–6	*Richard II*
1595–6	*Romeo and Juliet*
1595–6	*A Midsummer Night's Dream*

If Shakespeare had died in the plague of 1594, his name would be that of a promising playwright who had achieved less than Marlowe. However, the four plays he wrote for the reopened theatres are less crude, more conscious; their writing and shaping more careful and consistent. He had completed two accomplished long poems, and the new plays have richer poetic dimensions than their predecessors. Indeed, these four plays are sometimes called, for want of a better term, 'lyrical'. *Richard II* (discussed in the next chapter) is cast in a stately and plangent verse; the others (two comedies and a romantic tragedy) are mostly in blank verse but with much rhymed verse, some songs and sonnets, and, in their comic scenes, some prose. All four plays explicitly discuss language, and also verse and prose, alerting the audience to notice the different levels of style. They also discuss acting, to make the audience aware of its own collaborative role in the make-believe of theatre. These new plays are better than the plays of his contemporaries: more skilful, and in a language which creates a larger and more conscious world.

Table 1: Order of Composition

The chronology is conjectural, especially for the first plays. Later dates are firmer, but many remain approximate.

1589–92	*The Taming of the Shrew*	
1590–1	*The Two Gentlemen of Verona*	
1591	*2 Henry VI* and *3 Henry VI*	
1592	*1 Henry VI*	
1591–2	*Titus Andronicus*	[1592–3 *Venus and Adonis*]
1592–4	*Richard III*	[1593–4 *Lucrece*]
1594	*The Comedy of Errors*	[1593–1608 *Shake-speares Sonnets*]
1595	*Love's Labour's Lost*	
1595–6	*Richard II*	
	Romeo and Juliet	
1595–6	*A Midsummer Night's Dream*	
1595–7	*King John*	
1596–7	*The Merchant of Venice*	
1596–7	*1 Henry IV*	
1597–1601	*The Merry Wives of Windsor*	
1597–8	*2 Henry IV*	
1598	*Much Ado about Nothing*	
1599	*Henry V*	
	Julius Caesar	
	As You Like It	
1600–1	*Twelfth Night*	
	Hamlet	
1601–2	*Troilus and Cressida*	
1603–4	*Measure for Measure*	
1604	*Othello*	
1605	*All's Well that Ends Well*	
	Timon of Athens	
1605–6	*King Lear*	
1605–6	*Macbeth*	
1606–7	*Antony and Cleopatra*	
1607–8	*Pericles*	
	Coriolanus	
1609–11	*The Winter's Tale*	
1610–11	*Cymbeline*	
1611	*The Tempest*	
1613	*Henry VIII* (with John Fletcher)	
1613–14	*The Two Noble Kinsmen* (with John Fletcher)	

Table 2: Chronology of Publication

Thirty-six plays were collected and published in *Mr. William Shakespeares Comedies, Histories, & Tragedies*, the edition of 1623 known as the First Folio (F1). At Shakespeare's death in 1616, 18 plays had appeared in Quarto format. A Quarto (Q) is a small, unbound book, like a modern paperback, retailing at sixpence. The Folio is a large thick book, its pages twice the size, with two columns of text to the page. It sold at one pound sterling, 40 times as much as a Quarto; the buyer would then pay for it to be given a leather binding.

The Quartos, listed in order of printing, with the dates of later Quarto editions:

1593	*Venus and Adonis*	16 further Qs to 1636
1594	*Lucrece*	8 further Qs
1594	*2 Henry VI*	1600, 1619
1595	*3 Henry VI*	
1595	*Titus Andronicus*	1600, 1611
1597	*Romeo and Juliet*	1599, 1609, 1622?, 1637
1597	*Richard II*	1598, 1598, 1603, 1608, 1615, 1634
1597	*Richard III*	1598, 1602, 1605, 1622, 1629, 1634
1598	*1 Henry IV*	1598, 1598, 1599, 1604, 1608, 1613, 1622, 1632, 1639
1598	*Love's Labour's Lost*	1631
1600	*2 Henry IV*	
1600	*The Merchant of Venice*	1619, 1637
1600	*A Midsummer Night's Dream*	1619
1600	*Much Ado about Nothing*	
1600	*Henry V*	1602, 1619
1602	*The Merry Wives of Windsor*	1619, 1630
1603	*Hamlet*	1604, 1605, 1625, 1637
1608	*King Lear*	1619
1609	*Shake-speares Sonnets*	
1609	*Troilus and Cressida*	
1609	*Pericles*	1611, 1619, 1629
1622	*Othello*	1630
1623	First Folio: *Mr. William Shakespeares Comedies, Histories, & Tragedies*	
1631	*The Taming of the Shrew*	
1632	Second Folio	
1634	*The Two Noble Kinsmen* (with John Fletcher; not in F1)	

Venus and Adonis and *Lucrece*, printed before any play, were reprinted more often than any play, perhaps due to their erotic subject matter. Thereafter most new plays were published in Quarto until *Hamlet*. Only four plays composed after 1603 were printed in Quarto before 1623. Thirteen later plays first appeared in the Folio, as did five earlier plays. There were more readers for history than tragedy, more readers for tragedy than comedy.

Comedy and history predominate over tragedy in Shakespeare's early career: kinds of play more open and inclusive than tragedy. Comedy came readily to him – half of his plays are comedic – and his earlier critics, from Jonson to Johnson, preferred his comedy, finding his tragedy over-written.

Love's Labour's Lost

The skilfulness of the first three comedies does not prepare us for the wit and brio of *Love's Labour's Lost* and the four-level plot of *A Midsummer Night's Dream*. The first of these poetic plays, *Love's Labour's Lost*, opens with the following lines, spoken by the King of Navarre to his friends:

> Let fame, that all hunt after in their lives
> Live register'd upon our brazen tombs
> And then grace us in the disgrace of death,
> When, spite of cormorant devouring Time,
> The endeavour of this present breath may buy
> That honour which shall bate his scythe's keen edge,
> And make us heirs of all eternity. ...
>
> Our late edict shall strongly stand in force;
> Navarre shall be the wonder of the world;
> Our court shall be a little academe,
> Still and contemplative in living art.
>
> (1.1.1–7; 11–14)

The writing here has the firm metrical regularity and declamatory vigour of the history plays, but a quieter eloquence. The king's ardent fanfare strikes the notes of Shakespeare's early Sonnets: fame, present breath, honour, eternity, life, death, brazen tombs, and cormorant devouring Time with his keen scythe. These are Shakespeare's variants on the terms in which Renaissance humanist poetry aspired to literary immortality, in the verse of Petrarch in Italian, Ronsard in French, Sidney and Spenser in English. Shakespeare owed much not just to English playwrights but also to the non-dramatic prose and poetry of his predecessors and contemporaries in several languages: in English, to Chaucer, Gower, Sidney, Spenser and the sonneteers, as well as to Holinshed, to many a prose romance, and to the Elizabethan translators of Seneca, Ovid, Plutarch and Montaigne. His own literary ambitions are articulated here with a dramatist's confidence, projection and sense of occasion.

The initial situation of *Love's Labour's Lost*, however, lacks the solemnity of some humanist literary theory. There is also in Navarre's voice a festive note, characteristic of the play as a whole, as he announces to his three young companions his new and splendid idea: that they join him for three years in studying wisdom, at the end of which they will know how to live well. Such an idea of a university had influenced the Florentine court of Lorenzo de' Medici in the fifteenth century. Navarre proposes that this new Platonic and Pythagorean Academy will forswear not only meat but also the company of ladies. Five minutes later, a company of ladies arrives and the men immediately fall for them. The contemplative academe becomes a competitive court of love as the philosopher kings try to win the hearts of a diplomatic delegation conveniently consisting of a Princess of France, three young ladies-in-waiting and an old counsellor.

As the play's title suggests, love's labour is to be lost: no love, no Platonic philosophy, only the lessons of experience. Shakespeare had probably read of such a noble academy in de la Primaudaye's *L'académie francaise*. But the idea that life can be learned from books, together with a set of courtiers wooing with repetitive poetic eloquence and no success, is to be found in Chaucer's *Parliament of Fowls*, a courtly work with comical lower orders, in which all the speakers are birds. In the play, as in Chaucer's *Parliament*, serial wooing ends with a noble female sending three noble lovers away for a year. Both works also end with the singing of birds. Accompanying the ballet of four young couples is a Mozartian subplot of Dull, Costard, and a fantastical Don Adriano, a Spaniard smitten with the country wench Jaquenetta. There is good rustic humour, of which one exchange will suffice: Adriano: 'I love thee.' Jaquenetta: 'So I heard you say' (1.2.130).

In *Love's Labour's Lost* the men fall in love but dare not tell each other; the ladies disguise themselves and make the men look foolish. The men's decision to break their vows is rationalised by the witty Biron (who appears as 'Berowne' in some editions):

> From women's eyes this doctrine I derive.
> They sparkle still the right Promethean fire.
> They are the books, the arts, the academes
> That show, contain and nourish all the world.
>
> (4.3.325–8)

After an Interlude of the Nine Worthies, put on by the non-noble characters, news comes of the death of the Princess's father. These very amateur dramatics end not in four weddings but in a funeral and a year's mourning. The men try to continue their wooing but are repulsed; Biron is reminded by his lady Rosaline that 'A jest's prosperity lies in the ear / Of him that hears it, never in the tongue / Of him that makes it.' She sends him to do charitable work, and 'jest a twelve-month in a hospital' (5.2.843–5; 853). The play ends with the Cuckoo's song of Spring, answered by the Owl's song of Winter. It is an English winter:

> When icicles hang by the wall,
>   And Dick the shepherd blows his nail,   *on his finger-nails*
> And Tom bears logs into the hall,
>   And milk comes frozen home in pail,
> When blood is nipped, and ways be foul,
> Then nightly sings the staring owl:
>   'Tu-whit, Tu-whoo!' – A merry note,
> While greasy Joan does keel the pot.   *cool*
>
> When all aloud the wind doth blow
>   And coughing drowns the parson's saw   *sermon*
> And birds sit brooding in the snow,
>   And Marian's nose looks red and raw,
> When roasted crabs hiss in the bowl   *crab-apples*
> Then nightly sings the staring owl:
>   'Tu-whit, Tu-whoo!' – A merry note,
> While greasy Joan doth keel the pot.

This 'conceited comedy' is carried off by a play of language and ideas so high-spirited that its sudden stop, the loss of love's labour in death, is a shock. After the gallantry and laughter, the black clothes of the Messenger announce his news before he tells it to the Princess. At the outset, Biron had used words to puncture the King's dream. To make action comment upon words thus, at the climax, shows a mastery of theatre. Death stops the dance, and the dismissal of love's labourers is followed by the mocking cuckoo and the wintry owl.

Rosaline is the first typically Shakespearian heroine – a woman of sounder understanding than the witty man who swears love to her. Romantic love is folly, but a necessary folly; for foolish mistakes are the way to learning. Biron: 'Let us once lose our oaths to find ourselves / Or else we lose ourselves to keep our oaths' (4.3.336–7).

Romeo and Juliet

The stage potential of *Love's Labour's Lost* was rediscovered only in the twentieth century, whereas *Romeo and Juliet*, seemingly composed in the following year, has had regular revivals. The plays deal with the literary conventions to do with young love, but differently. The comedy in the first half of the love tragedy *Romeo and Juliet* is realistically edgy and uneasy, and the second half rushes blackly to its tragic catastrophe. Young love between the children of old enemies, ending in tears, is an ancient theme; several versions of the story were known to Shakespeare. In this case, the play closes with the bereaved fathers of Romeo and Juliet promising to end the feud between Capulets and Montagues which has stained the streets of Verona.

This is a play which is often studied at school by pupils who are older than Juliet and Romeo. In love comedy, sympathy lies with the very young rather than with the fathers trying to find rich and suitable husbands for their daughters. Shakespeare's sympathies are inclusive – Tybalt may be an exception – but sympathy can be critical. The lovers of the title are the focus of attention, but the rapturous love that possesses them is not presented with simple rapture. If the opening street-fighting scene shows the stupidity of blind partisanship, a comparable blindness afflicts Romeo, whose supposedly fatal love for Rosaline is shown to be fatuous as soon as he sees Juliet. Romeo is as dominated by Cupid as Tybalt is by Mars. Love's blindness is proverbial, and can (in tragedy) have results quite as fatal as those of blind hatred. Limited vision is not confined to the young; affection leads Capulet, the Nurse and the kindly, well-meaning Friar into unwise counsels. The play is full of symmetrical contrasts – between Montague and Capulet, between old and young, and in the elaborate patterns of the words, as in a sonnet. Symmetries such as these may be more visible to a reader than to an audience. An overview also shows a pattern in the play's structure: the Prince who opens and closes the play also presides at its midpoint, when comedy tips into tragedy with the death of Mercutio.

There is plenty of 'low' material to reduce the excesses of the lovers' exaltation – and the lovers themselves are not the kings and queens of tragedy. Yet it remains unclear how to take the melodramatic arias of lamentation over the death of Tybalt, lamentations repeated at Juliet's first (apparent) death. The exclamations over her supposed corpse verge on the comic, especially those of the Nurse, and the appearance of the musicians comes as a relief. This makes the final tragedy, the actual deaths of Romeo and then of Juliet, more unrelieved; they take place in an appalled hush. Shakespeare is learning how to play upon the feelings of the audience.

The Nurse, in Shakespeare's time played by a boy or a man, is today a gift to an experienced actress. She is the first of a string of humorous characters, stock types transformed by Shakespeare into believable speakers; we are soon to meet Bottom, Falstaff and Mistress Quickly. Old Capulet, too, is shrewdly drawn: the crotchety, humorous master of a household, very much older than his 28-year-old wife; kindly till crossed; then enraged, absurd. The Nurse is garrulous, inconsequential, doting and slightly mad; overflowing with folk humour about reproduction. Her river of talk, reminiscent, repetitive, almost idiotic, is in absolute contrast to the tense speech of almost everyone else the play, a contrast and a relief. It comes as a shock, then, when this affectionate and devoted servant counsels her dear Juliet to take the Count Paris, not the Romeo whose suit the Nurse had furthered and favoured. But the Nurse is a servant retained in the house of the Capulets, and Romeo is a Montague; she is frightened.

The play has justly famous central scenes between boy and girl, especially at the dawn exchange before they must part. Juliet: 'It was the nightingale and not the lark / That pierc'd the fearful hollow of thine ear' (3.5.2–3). Their love carries traditional baggage: a set of paradoxes and commonplaces found in Petrarch, Chaucer and Elizabethan sonnets, heartfelt but predictable. To these Shakespeare adds the series of one-line exchanges known as stichomythia, and much melodrama. The plot at first seems rather silly, but it gathers speed from Act 3 onwards and rushes pell-mell to a bloody conclusion: first Mercutio and Tybalt, then Romeo, Juliet, Paris and Lady Montague, a conclusion which offers the strange satisfactions of tragedy.

A Midsummer Night's Dream

Shakespeare raises his game to new heights of invention in *A Midsummer Night's Dream*, and the play therefore receives extended attention. Duke Theseus of Athens is to wed the Amazon Queen, Hippolyta; two young Athenian couples, after much confusion in a wood near Athens, also marry. The King and Queen of the Fairies, Oberon and Titania, quarrel passionately over an Indian boy; Oberon makes Titania fall in love with Bottom, a weaver who (in another part of the wood) rehearses with his friends a play for the Duke's wedding. (Shakespeare, the son of a tradesman from a small town in the Forest of Arden, was now a member of the Lord Chamberlain's Men, playing in his own creations before the highest in the land.) The play, unlike *Love's Labour's Lost* and *Romeo and Juliet*, ends with three weddings – and Titania and Oberon reconciled.

The source for the Athenian part of the story is Chaucer's Knight's Tale; Shakespeare adds to the triangle of young lovers a second woman, in love with a man who scorns her. A foursome permits a comedy ending without loss of life. Puck, servant to the fairy gods Oberon and Titania, is a creature from English folklore. As in *Love's Labour's Lost*, the subplot characters are portraits from life, and recognisably English. Bottom and his friends, straight from the streets of Stratford, choose to act an interlude of Pyramus and Thisbe, a love tragedy from Ovid's *Metamorphoses*. Metamorphosis means change of shape, and Bottom is transformed into an ass, the main story in Apuleius' *Metamorphoses*, a Latin novel of the late second century, better known as *The*

Golden Ass. The introduction of a non-Christian god and goddess into a modern milieu takes a hint from Chaucer's Merchant's Tale. With great assurance, Shakespeare choreographs these incongruous and disparate elements into an action on four levels: fairy king and queen, legendary hero and heroine, fashionable young lovers, and English tradesmen. In this dream, four worlds seem to hang together quite naturally. Shakespeare mixes his eclectic reading into an entertainment which is dazzlingly light but has its depths. Optional depth was to become one of his specialities.

Directed by Oberon, Puck puts an ass's head on Bottom, and squeezes the love-inducing juice of a magic herb onto Titania's eyelid. She wakes and loves the first creature she sees – the asinine Bottom, whom she carries off to her bower. The love-juice causes operatic silliness among the four young lovers in the wood. But Jack shall have Jill: Oberon makes Puck put everything right in time for the Duke's wedding. The wedding-eve of the Duke (and of the lovers) is filled up with the play of Pyramus and Thisbe, lovers who, each convinced the other is dead, commit suicide. The innocent artisans' efforts at tragedy are met by the laughter of the court; and audiences always laugh at the lovers' suicide: 'very tragical mirth'. It is a brilliantly unsuitable play for a wedding. Shakespeare had used a strikingly similar tragedy of errors to end his immediately previous play, *Romeo and Juliet*. He may well have been working on the two plays at the same time, and there is much crossover and reversal in the plots.

If comedy is tragedy averted, it is often in Shakespeare averted narrowly. The passions of the lovers in the wood are conventionally expressed and interchangeable. This sameness is deliberate – as Benjamin Britten brings out well in his opera of the play, where the four voices sing duets of love and hate, which turn into a final harmonious ensemble. The fierce jealousy of the fairies is expressed in a sumptuous poetry, while the irrationality of sexual possession is suggested only lightly in the love of the classically named goddess Titania for Bottom. The unimaginative Bottom says at 4.2.206, waking up:

> I have had a most rare vision. I have had a dream past the wit of
> man to say what dream it was. Man is but an ass if he go about t'
> expound this dream. Methought I was – there is no man can

tell what. Methought I was, and methought I had – but man is but a patched fool if he will offer to say what methought I had. The eye of man hath not heard, the ear of man hath not seen, man's hand is not able to taste, his tongue to conceive, nor his heart to report what my dream was. I will get Peter Quince to write a ballad of this dream. It shall be called 'Bottom's Dream', because it hath no bottom ....

'Bottom's dream' in a Warwickshire voice sounds the same as 'bottomless dream'. The earthy Bottom puts his enjoyment of the fairy queen in terms that parody St Paul on the unimaginability of Heaven (1 Corinthians 2:9). Dreams of love on a warm but moonlight night are the subject of the play. Hippolyta opens Act 5: ''Tis strange, my Theseus, that these lovers speak of.' Theseus replies:

> More strange than true. I never may believe
> These antique fables nor these fairy toys.
> Lovers and madmen have such seething brains,
> Such shaping fantasies, that apprehend
> More than cool reason ever comprehends.
> The lunatic, the lover, and the poet
> Are of imagination all compact.
>
> ... And as imagination bodies forth
> The forms of things unknown, the poet's pen
> Turns them to shapes, and gives to airy nothing
> A local habitation and a name ...
>
> (5.1.2–8; 14–17)

To the cool Athenian reason of Theseus, the story of the night is incredible; to Hippolyta it testifies to something real:

> But all the story of the night told over,
> And all their minds transfigured so together,
> More witnesseth than fancy's images,
> And grows to something of great constancy;
> But, howsoever, strange and admirable.
>
> (5.1.24–8)

They exchange roles in their reactions to the Interlude:

Hippolyta: This is the silliest stuff that ever I heard.
Theseus: The best in this kind are but shadows [actors], and
               the worst are no worse if imagination amend them.
Hippolyta: It must be your imagination, then, and not theirs.
Theseus: If we imagine no worse of them than they of them-
               selves, they may pass for excellent men.

                                                      (5.1.212–17)

We can learn much from this long and complex scene and from
this pair of exchanges, one verse, one prose, about Shakespeare's
idea of theatre. The play-within-the-play, first staged in *Love's
Labour's Lost*, became a favoured device, used to great effect in
Hamlet. It functions like a mirror placed in a Renaissance painting,
showing the subject from two angles, and bringing the spectator
into the room. The players become spectators; the playhouse audience are spectators, godlike, but aware that they too are visible to
higher powers. Hippolyta, who had found truth in dreams, cannot
accept the play of the mechanicals; whereas her rational lord, who
doubted the dream and thinks of poets as mad, lends his imagination to complete the players' inadequacies. Are dream and play the
same? Can either be trusted?

That all the world's a stage, and all the men and women merely
players, as Jaques says in *As You Like It*, was a common conceit.
A poem by Walter Raleigh puts it neatly:

What is our life? a play of passion,
Our mirth the musicke of division;   *accompaniment*
Our mothers' wombs the tiring-houses be,   *dressing rooms*
Where we are drest for this short Comedy.
Heaven the judicious sharp spectator is,
That sits and marks still who doth act amiss,   *constantly observes*
Our graves that hide us from the searching sun
Are like drawn curtains when the play is done.
Thus march we playing to our latest rest,
Only we die in earnest – that's no jest.

A Midsummer Night's Dream and *Romeo and Juliet* make a profitable comparison. Sexual attraction is irresistible, arbitrary and (in comedy) benign, leading to marriage for human lovers, young and old. The loves of the fairy king and queen, however, are more absurdly irrational and self-indulgent, as in the jealous quarrel over the Indian toy-boy and the spectacle of beauty doting upon a beast. In the love tragedy, the same attraction, though presented with empathy, is irresistible, arbitrary and fatal – leading, through a series of mistakes, to the lovers' suicide. The tragic pathos of this outcome was to be parodied in the suicide of Pyramus and Thisbe, and in Pyramus/Bottom's farcical dying speech:

> 'Come, tears, confound:
> Out, sword, and wound
> The pap of Pyramus;
> Ay, that left pap,
> Where heart doth hop.   [*Stabs himself*
> Thus die I, thus, thus, thus.
> Now am I dead,
> Now am I fled;
> My soul is in the sky,
> Tongue, lose thy light;
> Moon, take thy flight.   [*Exit Moonshine*
> Now die, die, die, die, die.'
>   (5.1.297–308)

6
Histories

Of all Shakespeare's plays, only four have plots which originate with him: *Love's Labour's Lost*, *A Midsummer Night's Dream*, *The Merry Wives of Windsor* and *The Tempest*. These are comedies, and there are written sources for parts of them. But the ten English histories, although taken from the prose chronicles of Holinshed and others, are, as a group, a most original achievement on a very large scale, feeding the Elizabethans' appetite for plays about the turbulent history of their country. Shakespeare's histories convert the chronicles' often ramshackle historical narratives into drama of high quality. These history plays have also had far more offspring than Shakespeare's comedy and tragedy, giving England an abstract and brief chronicle of its ideas of late medieval England, and providing a prototype for Walter Scott's invention of the historical novel, and for all the historical fiction that has followed Scott.

Shakespeare is sometimes said to have invented the history play, but it is truer to say that he brought a new and simple genre to a high state of perfection. This is not to belittle his Greek and Roman histories (classed in the Folio as tragedies), but there had been such classical plays before. Shakespeare wrote ten English histories in all, listed in the Folio in the order of the reigns of the kings in their titles. The reign order was not the order of composition. The first tetralogy was written in 1590–3:

First history plays

1591	*2 Henry VI*
1591	*3 Henry VI*
1592	*1 Henry VI*
1592–4	*Richard III*

We shall look at the second tetralogy, composed in 1595–9:

Second set of history plays

1595–6	*Richard II*
1596–7	*1 Henry IV*
1597–8	*2 Henry IV*
1599	*Henry V*

Shakespeare's reigns-on-stage stop with the overthrow of King Richard III and the advent of the Tudor dynasty. As Shakespeare began writing, Elizabeth authorised the execution of Mary Queen of Scots, the mother of the man who was to succeed her, James VI of Scotland. Dynastic historiography was dangerous. From 1547 the Tudors made sure that their subjects heard regularly from the pulpit about their duty to obey the Crown. Church attendance was the law, and nine times a year homilies were read on the divine appointment of kings and the duty of subjects to order and obedience. Ten years after Elizabeth's death Shakespeare could collaborate on a *Henry VIII* in which the portrayals of Sir Thomas More and of Katherine of Aragon are sympathetic – and Elizabeth is eulogised.

Shakespeare's histories draw on the 1587 *Chronicles* of Holinshed, and on plays such as *Woodstock*, about the murder of Thomas of Woodstock, uncle of Richard II. The danger of writing history plays is illustrated by the story of the Earl of Essex's attempt to overthrow Elizabeth. On the afternoon before Essex's attempted coup in 1601, his supporters commissioned a special performance of *Richard II*. Shakespeare's company put it on, later testifying to their reluctance and saying that the play was stale. The Queen remarked of this that it had been played 40 times (since, that is, 1595). It was not stale to her, as is shown by the sharpness of her recorded reaction: 'I am Richard the Second, know ye not that?'

As a monarch, she identified with Richard as a king deposed and done away with – on the order of an ancestor from whom she traced her indirect and disputed claim to the throne. The security services had in any case penetrated the Essex plot, and Essex was executed. But Elizabeth's 'know ye not that?' makes it clear that anything can be given a political or personal application. Hamlet's saying that something is rotten in the state of Denmark could be taken as applying to England; Shakespeare could deny that he meant any such thing, but Hamlet catches the conscience of a king with a play. Even a dumb show can be dangerous.

Richard II

Richard II is an historical tragedy modelled on Marlowe's *Edward II* in its set-up and its manipulation of audience sympathies. In each play the ruler's irresponsibility and unfitness is clear, but once he is deposed we are made to pity him. Edward neglects his country for the company of the low-born Gaveston; Edward's noble opponents are less likeable even than he; his wife and son conspire against him. *Edward II* shows the unedifying workings of power, relieved by the flares of homosexual infatuation. After a red-hot poker and screams, Marlowe's play closes with the young Edward III, a figure of order. But in such history there is little moral significance.

In marked contrast, *Richard II* is rich in poetry and in ideas. Through John of Gaunt, Duke of Lancaster, Shakespeare provides a poetry of England as a Christian kingdom, this 'other Eden', this 'blessed plot', though watered with the blood and tears of civil war. The king is 'the deputy anointed by the Lord', and the play is symbolic, sacramental, symphonic. It opens with mutual chivalric defiance (which Richard calls off, exiling the combatants) and continues with formal, ceremonial verse almost throughout. The keynote is Gaunt's dying vision of medieval England as it ought to be, and then as it currently is, leased out to Richard's tax-farming cronies. 'Time-honoured' Lancaster's feudal music ends with his death; Richard smartly announces that 'we seize into our hands, / His plate, his goods, his money and his lands' (2.1.209–10). The disinheriting of Lancaster's son, Henry Bolingbroke, strikes down the principle of succession by which the king holds his throne, and gives the returning Bolingbroke the perfect slogan for his march through England: 'I come for Lancaster' (2.3.113). He comes also for England.

Action is symbolic and symmetrical. Richard weeps to stand upon his kingdom once again, but sits to hear sad stories of the death of kings; the sun rises, but Richard, whose symbol is the sun, falls: 'down, down I come, like glistering Phaethon, / Wanting the manage of unruly jades' (3.3.177–8). He has a series of arias lamenting his fall, deploying the sacred language which at Gaunt's bedside had made him yawn. At Flint Castle, the crossover point, Richard has to 'come down' to the aspiring Bolingbroke, likened to two buckets in a well: one going down empty, the other going up full. There follow the symbolic garden scene, and the self-deposition scene, arranged in Westminster Hall, so that Henry may 'proceed without suspicion' – a scene cut from the 1598 Quartos as too politically dangerous. Henry says that 'in God's name' he ascends the royal throne. The Bishop of Carlisle bravely points out that he lacks God's blessing, which Henry concedes. He deals with quarrelling nobles firmly, unlike the petulant Richard of Act I. Henry ends the play with a vow to go as a pilgrim to Jerusalem to purge the guilt of Richard's murder. An efficient pragmatist succeeds 'the Lord's anointed,' a title Richard uses of himself. (Since 973, when Archbishop Dunstan anointed Edgar before crowning him king, English monarchs have been anointed before they are crowned – as Samuel anointed David in the name of the Lord as King of Israel.) Richard invoked divine sanctions and did nothing; the usurper uses the language of rights and does not put a foot wrong. The end has justified the means, but the 'silent king' cannot now invoke the old sanctions; and he finds that he cannot sleep.

Richard II is a foundation for the three-play sequence topped out by *Henry V*. Shakespeare took care with the foundations: *Richard II* draws on seven different sources, including Marlowe's *Edward II*, and goes beyond them. It is a tragedy, but Richard is not a noble tragic hero; he likens his passion to Christ's, but we pity him less than he pities himself. Shakespeare, however, did not observe the tragic norms which Renaissance theorists derived from Aristotle. History is raw and untidy, and has to be cooked and given a dramatic shape. Also, as Sidney noted, history shows that the wicked prosper, although Shakespeare's Chronicle sources had sometimes also found in it signs of providential design. The purpose of the tetralogy is revealed by the dying speech of Henry IV, who tells his son that 'the soil of the achievement [the guilt of usurpation] / Goes with me into the earth' (*2 Henry IV*, 4.3.318–19): his son's succession is 'plain and right'. Henry V, the hero of Agincourt, paved the way for the Tudors. He married Katharine of France, brought her to England and died, whereupon she married Owen Tudor, the grandfather of Henry VII, Elizabeth's grandfather. Shakespeare writes from within the traditions of what was later called the (pro-Lancastrian) 'Tudor myth'.

Henry IV

The depth and width of Shakespeare's resources is shown in the first and second parts of *Henry IV*, and in *Henry V*, plays very different from the all-verse *Richard II*. They mingle verse and prose, high and low, court and tavern, royal camp and rebel camp in a many-sided representation of the life of England. Falstaff's first words, 'Now, Hal, what time of day is it, lad?' (1.2.1), create character as decisively as Henry's opening line, 'So shaken as we are, so wan with care' (1.1.1). Falstaff's hangover, his impudent familiarity with his Prince, and his neglect of time are Theme as well as Character. Shakespeare turns to profit the problem of Hal's legendary wild youth by creating a gloriously attractive if entirely irresponsible drinking companion in Falstaff. Prince Hal studies the common people he will have to lead in war; he learns their ways and speech, and the part he will have to play. The rebel Hotspur scorns 'this king of smiles, this Bolingbroke' and his efforts at 'popularity'. But acting is now part of political life: Henry IV sends into the battlefield at Shrewsbury men dressed as himself, duplicate kings whom Douglas kills. These multiplied images admit that the monarchy has lost its sacredness, that kingship is a role, with Hal as understudy. Hal transforms into Prince Henry at Shrewsbury, kills the honourable Hotspur and, as in a fairy tale, allows Falstaff to take the credit. We have seen Falstaff stab Hotspur's dead body, but Shakespeare has worked a trick whereby Hal has touched pitch and is not defiled, and the morally unattractive Falstaff remains fictionally attractive.

In the second part of *Henry IV* we see less of Hal and less of the comic and festive side of unruly popular life, more of its disease and low tricks. We also see trickery and suspicion in high places, and some slippery high politics. Already in the first part we have heard Hotspur's tart comment on the promises of princes: 'The King is kind; and well we know the King / Knows at what time to promise, when to pay' (4.3.54–5). In the second part, Prince John cheats; King Henry wrongly accuses Prince Henry of wanting him dead so that he can take the crown. In their last interview he advises his son to 'busy giddy minds / With foreign quarrels' – a Machiavellian tip often taken by subsequent leaders, and one which casts an unglamorous light upon Agincourt (5.1.214–15). We hear Falstaff excuse his recruitment of soldiers who are physically unable to fight – Mouldy, Shadow, Wart and Feeble – on the ground that as 'Food for powder, food for powder; they'll fill a pit as well as better' (4.2.65). The rogues of Eastcheap will serve in *Henry V* as a foil to a nobler king. In a rich invention, Mr Justice Shallow in his Gloucestershire orchard reminisces with Falstaff about their naughty youth, and how their days of wenching and boozing will return when Falstaff is Lord Chief Justice. Falstaff does not join in these fantasies. When he publicly accosts the new king as he comes from his crowning, he is banished and repudiated – 'I know thee not, old man' (5.5.47). This lovable Vice was to ride again in *The Merry Wives of Windsor*.

Henry V

Henry V begins in a new way by telling us that it is a literary chronicle turned into a play, set within 'this wooden O' (that is, the newly built Globe), with prologues and chorus and references to 'the story'. It is a pageant with heroic tableaux. Henry coolly plays his legendary role for all it is worth, but on the night before Agincourt we see him pray and suffer, and, in disguise as a common soldier, take the king's part in a justly celebrated discussion with common soldiers. We see him dealing with nobles, traitors, enemies, soldiers, captains, the French court, the Princess. Like his father, he hardly puts a foot wrong in his enterprise, which, like his father's, is of debatable legality. The son, however, unlike the father, is able to obtain clerical approval before he acts. As king, Henry never meets the denizens of Eastcheap, and Falstaff dies offstage.

Throughout *Henry V* we see the seamy side of the tapestry of history alternate with the public side, and are shown how words differ from deeds. Pistol's boastful misappropriation of language, mangling the ancient epic manner, has a comic relation to Henry's fine speeches at Agincourt. Immediately before the wooing of Kate of France we hear that Doll Tearsheet is dead and that Bardolph will run a brothel. The daughters of Harfleur are threatened with rape so that the town should yield; Kate learns English so that she may yield. Henry's clemency is followed by his angry killing of the prisoners, and a double-edged joke about 'Alexander the Pig' (a Welsh pronunciation of 'the Big', that is, the Great). The play is a carefully mounted study of how to be king, and of what it costs; but for all his courage and splendid words Henry is due respect rather than the unmerited love which animates the Hostess's account of the last of one of the 'gentleman in England now abed' of whom Henry speaks at Agincourt, Sir John Falstaff:

Mrs Quickly: Nay, sure he's not in hell. He's in Arthur's bosom, if ever man went to Arthur's bosom. A made a finer end, and went away an it had been any christom child. A parted ev'n just between twelve and one, ev'n at the turning o' th' tide – for after I saw him fumble with the sheets, and play with flowers, and smile upon his finger's end, I knew there was but one way. For his nose was as sharp as a pen, and a babbled of green fields. 'How now, Sir John?' quoth I. 'What, man! Be o' good cheer.' So a cried out, 'God, God, God', three or four times. Now I, to comfort him, bid him he should not think of God; I hoped there was no need to trouble himself with any such thoughts yet. So a bade me lay more clothes on his feet. I put my hand into the bed and felt them, and they were cold as any stone. Then I felt to his knees, and so up'ard and up'ard, and all was as cold as any stone. (2.3.25)

Shakespeare was a master of language but he delights in characters who are not: the vainglorious soldier, the pedantic schoolmaster, the Celt who appeals to ancestry and ancient precedent. Such windbags have theatrical precedent, but Shakespeare was the first to record the struggles between the English language and the police: Constable Dull is to be followed by several other agents of the law. We smile, but the final effect is more complex. Mistress Quickly says 'Arthur' for 'Abraham'; tells Falstaff that it is premature to think of God on his deathbed; and, as she tenderly feels up and up his legs, makes unfortunate use of 'cold as any stone' – a man's 'stones' were his testicles. (Here, a reader has the advantage of notes: an audience might miss 'stones', and might miss 'Arthur'.) Mistress Quickly's foolish heart is not well served by her tongue; she can hardly say what she means, yet we recognise the fondness in this farewell – fondness for a rogue who has consistently exploited it. Her motives, and her ability to speak sense, are far apart, and the onstage effect is different again. This is advanced dramatic writing.

The sacred ideals of England and of kingship, set up at the start of *Richard II* and turned into theatre by Richard at Flint Castle, were betrayed by him in practice. His usurping successor could not claim these ideals, firm and fair though his rule was. England is at last led to foreign victory by a king who succeeds by right, and who is shown to have well studied his people and his role. But the new relationship between England and her king is based on a providential combination of succession and success. As the Epilogue points out, Harry of Agincourt was too soon succeeded, as king of France and England, by the infant Henry VI, 'Whose state so many had the managing / That they lost France and made his England bleed' (11–12). This was a history which Shakespeare had already dramatised in *Henry VI* and *Richard III*.

In both artistic and human terms, Shakespeare's histories reach their penetrating best in *Henry IV*, a play which defies all norms of genre, mixing Henry's brooding distrust of his imprudent son with the comic irresponsibility of Eastcheap to produce a romance outcome: Hal's apparent wildness is made into Henry V's apprenticeship. The father–son conflict is rehearsed comically in Part 1, with Falstaff as King Henry, and in near-tragic earnest in Part 2. *1 Henry IV* was Shakespeare's most popular play for readers, to judge by the number of Quarto editions.

Comprehensiveness

Shakespeare shows a remarkable capacity to include all sorts and ranks in his historical presentation of a medieval England which is also the England of his own day, and human life in general. Such a comprehensiveness shows an older sense of human beings as unequal on earth but equal before God. This sense characterises medieval drama, William Langland's 'fair field full of folk', and Chaucer's Prologue to the *Canterbury Tales*, in which, as John Dryden wrote, 'God's plenty' is to be found. Renaissance dramatists wrote 'citizen comedies' which show a range of people, but all are from the urban middle class, with a country squire for contrast: a class which has since grown but is not the human norm. The quality of Shakespeare's representation of a very wide range of society, vertical and horizontal, is unequalled. It includes beggars, whores, outcasts (Poor Tom in *King Lear*), outsiders (such as a Jew and a Moor), tapsters, ostlers, household servants, children, tradesmen, shepherds, thieves, citizens, soldiers, generals, courtiers, ladies-in-waiting, kings and queens. If the quality is unequalled, the range is approached again later in Henry Fielding, Walter Scott, Charles Dickens and George Eliot.[1]

It has been said that to Shakespeare, as to Dickens, there was no such thing as an ordinary person, a compliment which points to a real quality of both. But characters in plays and novels differ from real persons; and theatre audiences, and the readers of popular fiction, have to be able quickly to identify what kind of person a new character is meant to be. Dramatists therefore usually begin with types which they individualise. Sir John Falstaff is partly the old Vice of the Morality plays, for example. It has also been suggested that he owes some traits – his girth, his wit and his dissipation – to the late Robert Greene.[2] Sir John's creator was a common man of uncommon gifts in a profession and a company which brought him into contact with every rank in society. His common touch grounds and universalises his later tragedies, especially the epic drama *King Lear*, which focuses on the plight of the outcast. In politics he seems to show that it is easier to fool a crowd than an individual.

Readers and dedicated theatregoers are able to consider these four history plays as a series; the second part of *Henry IV* depends somewhat on the first, but the others work well as independent plays. Shakespeare had written histories before this, which makes it pretty clear that as he prepared *Richard II* he was planning four plays, a tetralogy.

Versatility

It raises one's estimate of Shakespeare's abilities to know that he composed such a penetrating analysis of public life in regular alternation with the comedy he was also writing. Each year from 1596 to 1599, as the list below shows, brought a new comedy and a new history. After 1599 a different alternation begins, as history (using the Folio terms) begins to give way to tragedy.

Comedies and histories

1596–7	*The Merchant of Venice*
1596–7	*1 Henry IV*
1597–1601	*The Merry Wives of Windsor*
1597–8	*2 Henry IV*
1598	*Much Ado about Nothing*
1599	*Henry V*
1599	*Julius Caesar*
1599	*As You Like It*
1600–1	*Hamlet*
1600–1	*Twelfth Night*

This list shows that Shakespeare could write two different kinds of play almost at the same time. Greene was right to call him a *Johannes factotum*. He could do everything, and the alternating pattern of his writing career shows that he was ambidextrous. His plays before 1595 can be called comedies, histories or tragedies without raising false expectation. These genre ascriptions appear in the titles of many plays and gain authority in the title of the First Folio: *Mr William Shakespeares Comedies, Histories & Tragedies*. But after 1595, and notably in *The Merchant of Venice* (1596–7), Shakespeare begins to diversify, and generic expectation is less often met; the plays, after the opening-out of *Henry IV*, become multi-generic. *The Merchant*, nominally a comedy, is a tragicomedy showing an impassioned Jew baulked of his revenge. *The Merry Wives* is a farcical citizen comedy in which Falstaff rides again, in a laundry basket. *Much Ado* is a comedy but could equally be called a prose romance of a not very romantic kind. These are followed by two superior romance comedies, intellectually complex and emotionally subtle, the inventive pastoral *As You Like It* and the Italianate *Twelfth Night*. If we except *The Merry Wives*, all of these comedies are quite serious. In *The Merchant* and *Much Ado*, the comedy endings are snatched from tragedy in a way that drains their final reunions of any romance of an innocent kind. For this reason it now seems right, before proceeding to the second half of Shakespeare's career, to devote a chapter to one of these serious comedies.

7

The Merchant of Venice and the Whirligig of Time

This play appeared in print in 1600, with a title page reading *The most Excellent History of the Merchant of Venice. With the Extreame Cruelty of Shylocke the Iew towards the said Merchant, in cutting a just Pound of his flesh: And the obtaining of Portia, by choyse of three Chests. Written by W. Shakespeare*. On the next leaf, the play's story is introduced not as *most Excellent* but as *comicall*. History has since made its story less comical, which is why the play receives extended attention here.

The Merchant is not Shakespeare's most attractive play but it is perhaps the most obvious case of how changes in historical understanding affect how a play is perceived and understood, and how it is represented on the stage and in commentary. Its reception has been so altered by the Nazi attempt to exterminate European Jews that the original roots of the play's central conflict can be lost to view; this chapter hopes to show where they can be found.

Since an historical sense developed in the eighteenth century, educated opinion has approached works of the past historically, relating them, as far as it can, to their original context. But we also experience literary works as alive in the present moment, especially with a play. Evaluating a literary classic can be educative, leading to a better understanding of the work itself and of present-day attitudes. But in the case of *The Merchant of Venice* these perspectives are not easy to reconcile.

Formally, the play is a love comedy. It ends, as such comedy should, in marital unions; but this omits its darker and stronger half. The plot of *The Merchant* binds together two different kinds of story – one romantic, the other potentially fatal – each involving a trial. Audience curiosity is engaged in the outcomes of these trials: in one, a woman is bound to marry the suitor who chooses correctly between three caskets; in the other, a man binds himself, in an exceedingly unlikely eventuality, to give up one pound of his flesh to another man. Shakespeare makes the human interest of one of the stories into a major moral conflict. Speeches by Shylock and Portia embody and articulate themes of justice and mercy, resentment and forgiveness, law and grace.

The play is very often staged, the frequency of its performance rising with changes in how Judaism and Jews have been perceived. The merchant of the title is Antonio; Shylock the Jew is a moneylender.[1] Antonio borrows 3000 ducats from Shylock in order to support the suit of his prodigal young friend Bassanio, a candidate for the hand of Portia, a golden beauty, an heiress 'richly left'. Portia is to marry the suitor who chooses correctly between three caskets, as provided in her father's will, and Bassanio wants to make a good impression. Antonio trades in goods, Shylock in money. As the play opens, Antonio's fortune is invested in ships currently at sea, so he breaks the habit of a lifetime to help Bassanio by borrowing from Shylock; whose usurious taking of interest he has always condemned, even paying the debts of others who have defaulted on their interest payments to Shylock.

Most readers of this book will have heard more about the Jewish history of the last century than about Jewish–Christian relations in the centuries before *The Merchant* was written. The play cannot be properly understood without some idea of this pre-history, whereas what has happened since 1597 is strictly irrelevant to the play, while greatly affecting its reception. Christian–Jewish difference is originally religious. Jesus was a Jew and so were all his disciples. But whereas Judaism was racial, Christianity soon became non-racial and non-national, as Christ's apostles spread the Gospel to 'all nations', the non-Jewish 'Gentiles'. Shylock's speech prefix in the original printing is simply 'Iewe', and he speaks as standing for 'all my tribe' and for Judaism itself; he sees Antonio and the other Venetians simply as Christians. Religious and racial differences are first aroused by clearly conflicting attitudes to usury; but at the trial, Usury gives way to Justice and Mercy.

A more detailed account of the story is needed to serve as a basis for the discussion of historical changes in perspective. Shylock sees in Antonio's application for a loan a chance of revenge for Antonio's abuse of him. Shylock makes a fantastic proposal: a loan with no interest payments, but with a 'merry' penalty. Antonio signs a bond that says if he does not repay the ducats in three months, he will give a pound of his own flesh, to be cut from any part of his body that Shylock chooses.

Portia, the heiress of Belmont, an estate on the Venetian mainland, is to marry the suitor who chooses rightly between the three caskets, of gold, silver and lead – a fairy-tale condition as fantastic as the terms of Shylock's bond. Bassanio interprets the casket mottoes better than his noble but non-Venetian rivals. He chooses lead and wins gold, the hand of Portia, who is delighted. A letter arrives at Belmont saying that all Antonio's ships have miscarried, that he is ruined and will default on his loan. Bassanio the married man hurries to Venice to save Antonio.

In court before the Duke, Shylock demands his pound of flesh. Bassanio offers thrice the sum, with money which marriage has brought him. Shylock refuses, insisting on the pound of flesh named in the bond, and wins his case. He sharpens his knife, Antonio bares his breast, the scales are ready to weigh the pound of flesh.... But the Jew is adroitly baulked of his revenge by Balthazar, a young lawyer from Padua, who rules that Shylock may indeed carve out his pound of flesh – but not an ounce more nor an ounce less; nor may he take a drop of blood. Shylock then says he will take the money; but he is bound by his literalism to take his flesh but no blood, an impossible condition. Balthazar (who is Portia in disguise) now invokes another law, by which one who attempts the life of a citizen of Venice is liable to the death penalty. Shylock is given lesser penalties, which, however, include the obligation to become a Christian. Sick and defeated, he retires.

To the main plot Shakespeare, as usual in his comedy, adds another level by giving Bassanio and Portia lesser companions: upper servants or associates whose roles track those of the principals. Such parallels lead to comparison and assessment. Blonde Portia's black-haired gentlewoman Nerissa becomes engaged to Bassanio's noisy companion Gratiano. Bassanio and Gratiano break the promises exacted by their wives never to part with their wedding rings. Grateful to Balthazar for saving Antonio's life, they offer Balthazar and his clerk (Nerissa in disguise) whatever gifts they care to name. They ask for their own wedding rings, which, encouraged by Antonio, the men reluctantly give them. Earlier we have witnessed a very different engagement, as Shylock's daughter Jessica elopes with the Christian Lorenzo. Jessica is glad to fly the bondage of her father's house, stealing from him to finance her marriage to an 'unthrift' Venetian. The plot turns on bonds, fidelities, and written and verbal engagements to which penalties and rewards attach. The play constantly engages with the rival claims of justice and mercy. Divine justice and mercy, and their human manifestations, are often in tension in Jewish sacred scripture, the Old Testament of the Bible, and more prominent in the New Testament. A non-biblical entity, Fortune, is also involved at each turn of this lottery of a play, whether in the form of risk, of gold or of wealth.

Before the trial in Act 4, Shylock's daughter Jessica had fled with a diamond worth 2000 ducats, and a casket of ducats. By the end of the trial, Shylock, deprived of his revenge, must leave all he owns to this willing convert to the religion of his enemies, and can escape death only by conversion and loss of his religion. Act 5, in contrast to the traumas of Act 4, is light, cynically witty, operatically beautiful, and finally romantic – but the lightness has its sombre side, and the romance is secular and realistic. Shakespeare (who was investing his London earnings in Stratford property), makes it clear that Bassanio and Lorenzo begin as unthrifty adventurers, and end richly married. Bassanio wins a golden fleece: a blonde with a lot of gold. And both marriages are made possible by money either lent by or stolen from Shylock. Judaic tradition, imitated by Christians, had an 'Egyptian gold' principle, based on Exodus 3:22, which justified the borrowing or taking of gold from oppressors in order to devote it to sacred Jewish (or, by extension, Christian) ends; for God, as the commentators used to say, writes straight with crooked lines. Jehovah repeatedly does so in the life of Jacob, patriarch of the twelve tribes of Israel. Some such folk theology seems to play around the intricate plotting of *The Merchant of Venice*. The plot of a play may not meet the approval of an ethical rationalist.

Shakespeare liked to set plays in a mildly exotic Italy – in Verona, Padua, Mantua, Naples, Messina and Sicily. Five of his plays have a character called Antonio. His Roman plays and poems also have Italian locations. Most of these settings are nominal but Venice has a distinctive ethos. This city republic set in a lagoon was both like and unlike the island kingdom of England, and of special interest in London. The action of *The Merchant* takes place in the afternoon of Venetian power and influence. Things special to this watery city are mentioned. Shylock asks, 'What news on the Rialto?' Gossips report that 'in a gondola were seen together / Lorenzo and his amorous Jessica'. Portia tells a servant to 'Bring them ... to the traject, to the common ferry / Which trades to Venice'. Venice's unique constitution features also in Shakespeare's *Othello* (1604), which opens with a father losing a daughter, and an outsider on trial before a Duke of Venice. Merchants make money, and acquisitiveness is a theme in *The Merchant*. Ben Jonson's *Volpone* (1606) shows Venice as consumed by avarice and folly; his London comedies show a city consumed by folly and avarice. The trial in *The Merchant* opens with the stage direction *Enter the Duke, the magnificoes*. Ducats, the ducal coins of Venice, tinkle through the text.

The risk involved in Venetian commerce is highlighted in the opening speeches of the play. A speaker imagines the wreck of a merchant's cargo, whose ship would 'scatter all her spices on the stream' and 'Enrobe the roaring waters with my silks' (1.1.33–4). Spices and silks, profitable Eastern imports, came to Venice by sea. Spice improves food, silk improves the looks of the wearer. Luxury was a favourite target of contemporary preachers, but the focus here is on the waste: the wreck imagined at the play's outset shows silks and spices swallowed by the sea. Shakespeare's imagery for Venice, which recalls the gorgeous silks of Titian and the wealth shown in Veronese's paintings, also shows its prosperity as fickle. Fittingly, though this is not mentioned in the play, the golden figure on top of Venice's customs house, through which all her trade passed, is Fortuna, an elegant weathervane.

The money-making Venice of the play has an atmosphere both bored and excitable, like wealthy New York in films of the late twentieth century. London and Venice prospered through trade, but Venice was richer, less provincial, more glamorous. Today

Venice is a shell, a relic; yet in 1597 Venice still had an empire and England had nothing outside the British Isles. Antonio has ships trading to Tripolis, Barbary, Lisbon, England, Mexico and India. Venice has a sea empire and a land empire: its merchants make money on the Rialto amid the lagoon and relax on mainland estates such as Belmont. Its republic under an elected Doge (in the play a Duke) was as ancient as England's monarchy. Venice's Arsenal (shipyard) of shipping and its marine finance and insurance made it the embarkation point for crusade and pilgrimage, the West's port for the East – and also its bulwark against the Turk, with whom it neverthless traded. It was the religious crossroads of Europe, where the old East–West schism dividing Latin Catholic and Greek Orthodox (now ruled by Turkey) met the recent North–South divisions of the Reformation. Venice accepted foreign traders from the Mediterranean and beyond: Orthodox, Protestant, Jew and Muslim. Bargains struck there were legally enforced against Venetian citizens. Venice was multiethnic, unlike England, a country from which, in 1290, the king had expelled Jews as misbelievers, repudiating also his own debts to them as usurers.

Why does Antonio so disapprove of Shylock? It has to do with money. The modern world lives on credit and on national debt, but the charging of interest for the use of money, known as usury, used generally to be held as a crime and a sin against nature. Jews are forbidden in Deuteronomy 23 to play the usurer with other Jews, but lending at interest to Gentiles was permitted; this had historic consequences. The charging of interest is banned in Islam and was strictly regulated in Christendom. Calvin permitted it, and London eventually followed Geneva, though Francis Bacon in his *Essay on Usury* (1625) maintained that it was 'against nature for money to beget money'.[2]

By reason, then, of its system of governance, its financial skill, and its commercial indifference to confessional allegiance, Venice was strange, a prodigy, an object of fascination to a London active in the exciting but morally dubious world of venture capital and finance. Venice had 'royal merchants', whereas England's aristocracy owned land, though in Shakespeare's lifetime its wealth had increasingly become commercial. *The Merchant* has the traditional Christian disapproval of avarice. Geoffrey Chaucer's Merchant boasts boringly of the gains he made in currency exchange, and Ben Jonson's *Volpone* (1606), also set in Venice, is about the dehumanising effects of avarice. It is said that Shakespeare's picture of Shylock aims at those English Puritans who used biblical texts to justify their making of money by lending money. Yet Shakespeare's dealings in Stratford show that, like his father before him, he charged interest on loans. Shakespeare's family background probably helped him to imagine the situation of those whose religion made them liable to pay fines, or, in extreme cases, to conform on pain of death. His plays show an increasing interest in extreme cases.

As the play opens, wealthy Christians are weary: Antonio 'knows not why [he is] so sad', and Portia, 'richly left', is bored at Belmont. Not so Shylock. Act 1, Scene 3 begins:

Shylock: Three thousand ducats, well.
Bassanio: Ay, sir, for three months.
Shylock: For three months, well.
Bassanio: For the which, as I told you, Antonio shall be bound.
Shylock: Antonio shall become bound, well.
Bassanio: May you stead me? Will you pleasure me? Shall I know your answer?
Shylock: Three thousand ducats for three months, and Antonio bound.
Bassanio: Your answer to that?
Shylock: Antonio is a good man.
Bassanio: Have you heard any imputation to the contrary?
Shylock: Ho no, no, no, no! My meaning in saying he is a good man is to have you understand me that he is sufficient. Yet his means are in supposition. He hath an argosy bound to Tripolis, another to the Indies ...

The audience had no list of the persons of the play, no theatre programme, none of the aids to understanding of modern editions of the text: character had to be created in a few strokes. Shylock's costume showed him as a Jew: costume signalled type, speech created role. Shylock's slow repetitions, marked idiom and accented speech rapidly impose a concentrated stage presence. Shylock repeats the wording of the requested loan, turning over its terms in his mouth as if testing them. A professional negotiator, he keeps Bassanio (and us) on the hook of uncertainty. Shylock explains to the green young gentleman that his statement 'Antonio is a good man' regards financial credit not moral credit. Antonio's money is all invested at sea, and Shylock weighs the chances of a default. Seeing a possibility, he finally says that he will take Antonio's bond, whereupon Bassanio invites him to 'dine with us'. Shylock: 'Yes, to smell pork, to eat of the habitation which your prophet the Nazarite conjured the devil into.' This insult sets alight the religious hostility which fuels half of the play.

Pork, for observant Jews, is polluting. Shylock alludes to the Gospel story of the Gadarene swine.[3] The Jew mocks the Christian belief that Jesus is the Son of God, pointing out also that Christians eat the unclean beast into which their 'prophet' sent devils. Yet Shylock conquers his disgust at what might be served at Christian tables: he chooses to go to Bassanio's, 'in hate to feed upon / The prodigal Christian' (2.5.24–5). When Shylock sees Antonio, his second line is 'I hate him for he is a Christian.' So Shylock hates Christians – and one can see why, since the Venetians abuse him until the end of the play. 'You call me misbeliever, cut-throat dog, / And spit upon my Jewish gaberdine', says Shylock to Antonio, who replies that he is like to do so again (1.3.108–9).[4] Shakespeare, who could make fun of a puritanical Malvolio, takes care to avoid the controversies which divided Christians. But he plants this play squarely on the fault line of Jewish–Christian antipathy.

Judaism was originally tribal, and is still so for Jews. Its law requires observant Jews to eat separately; strict Jews choose to live separately. But most people in Shakespeare's audience knew Jews only from hearsay. They would not knowingly have seen one, since Jews had been expelled from England in 1290, though a few came back. Jews were not officially allowed in England until 1655. Prejudice against them gradually declined until 1945, when the liberation of the Nazi death camps in 1945 exposed a prejudice which in England was by then more racial than religious. The anti-Jewish policy of the German National Socialist Party was entirely racial; for a true Nazi, all religion was weakness, Christianity included. In the eugenic theory adopted by the regime, inferior races, Gypsy or Jew, should be destroyed. Whether a Jew was observant, liberal, secular or Christian convert did not matter.

In reaction to the Shoah or Holocaust, well-intentioned modern productions of *The Merchant* in Britain often present the antagonism of Jew and Christian as racial. But the antagonism in this play is not simply racial: it originates in biblical differences that need to be recognised. Shakespeare knew his Bible, and knew something of modern Judaism. He shows the situation of a Jew with flashes of real sympathy, conceiving the character in reaction to Marlowe's caricature Jew, Barabas, the demonic trickster of *The Jew of Malta*, a play still being staged when *The Merchant* was first put on.[5]

More needs to be said about the biblical contexts which this text invokes, for they can be lost on those to whom they are unfamiliar. The adjective 'prodigal', for instance, is used four times in this play: by Shylock to Bassanio, quoted above; by Bassanio of his own carelessness with money (1.1.129); by Gratiano, as a noun meaning prodigal son (2.6.24); and again by Shylock, who at 3.1.41 calls Antonio 'a bankrupt, a prodigal'. In the parable of the prodigal son (in Luke 15), a young Jew wastes his inheritance and ends up feeding pigs in Egypt and eating their food, but then goes back to his father, who welcomes him. Those who do not know the parable miss crucial dimensions of this play. Another example is Shylock's first reaction on seeing Antonio: 'How like a fawning publican he looks' (1.3.40). In the New Testament a publican is not the landlord of an inn but a Jewish tax-farmer collecting taxes for the Romans: an oppressor, a traitor to his people. Publicans were shunned by other Jews, though Jesus was prepared to dine with them, and one of his parables prefers a humble publican to a proud Pharisee. Shylock next invokes Israel's origins in the book of Genesis, dwelling on Jacob, whom God gave a second name, Israel. Jacob son of Isaac, son of Abraham, is 'the third possessor' (1.3.71) of the promise made to the Jews. Jacob's sharp practice in outwitting his father-in-law, his blind father, and his elder brother made him the third Patriarch, the father of the twelve tribes of Israel. Shylock's wife is called Leah, like Jacob's first wife. So Shylock is not just a moneylender who approves of Jacob's guile: his racial pride makes him stand for ancient Israel.

His implacable and fierce personality makes Shylock Shakespeare's most powerful character so far. His King Richard III has crude diabolic energy, but theatrically is two-dimensional. And Richard is rarely off the stage, whereas Shylock appears in only five scenes, speaking fewer lines than the unmemorable Bassanio. He is a materialist – 'ships are but boards' (1.3.21) – cunning, vindictive and hard on his household. But he makes his varying passions felt. He softens when he hears of the turquoise ring stolen by Jessica and given in exchange for a monkey: 'I had it of Leah when I was a bachelor.' Always a compelling presence, we feel sympathy for him when we hear how Antonio is not ashamed to treat him. Sympathy for Shylock grew gradually in the eighteenth and nineteenth centuries in England, but sharply after 1945. His landmark speech, 'If you prick us, do we not bleed', is a direct and successful appeal to audience sympathy. But its climax, 'And if you wrong us, shall we not revenge? (3.1.61), is followed by an outburst in which Shylock swears that rather than his daughter marry a Christian, he would prefer her dead at his feet with the money in the coffin and her jewel in her ear. He prefers his ducats to his daughter, a phrase repeated by the boys of Venice; the words were then similar in pronunciation.

At the trial Portia reminds Shylock that 'The quality of mercy is not strained': the essence of mercy is that it is not constrained – not forced, not deserved, but freely given. Familiarity should not blunt the point of this speech. Mercy is the theme of the play: how mercy and love surpass justice; and specifically the retaliation which ancient Israel saw as righteous. Portia appeals to the reciprocal principle of the Lord's Prayer, a prayer that Christians know by heart: 'Forgive us our trespasses as we forgive those who have trespassed against us.' The people of England were obliged by law to attend church each Sunday, where they heard the prayer in the form which ends 'as we forgive our debtors'.[6] New Testament parables often turn on forgiving debtors. Antonio is Shylock's debtor, and clemency, not law, is what is at stake. Shylock appeals to law but wants revenge (3.1.361). Mutual clemency is a principle to which Shakespeare appeals again and again: in *Measure for Measure*; in *King Lear* when Lear and Cordelia kneel and exchange forgiveness, as Edgar and Edmund also do; in all four late romances. Forgiveness is fundamental to hope, and reconciliation is fundamental to comedy, as it is to all human living together. The play shows the strength of racial hatred, and takes us well beyond its limited perspectives. But a dislike of racism does not illuminate very much in this play: the religious differences need to be understood.

What is the origin of these differences? Paul, a zealous Jew, who had once persecuted Christians, taught that Gentile converts need not observe the ritual purities prescribed for Jews. Some Jews then persecuted Paul. Converts were soon mostly Gentiles, and Christianity began to distance itself from Judaism. Popular Christianity in medieval times forgot that the teaching of the Old Testament on justice and mercy gradually grew away from simple retaliation – 'an eye for an eye and a tooth for a tooth', the rule of tribal antiquity – towards mercy. Ancient Israel had always depended absolutely on God's mercy, as in the Psalms, Israel's book of common prayer: 'If thou, Lord, shouldest mark us according to our iniquities, O Lord, who shall stand?' (Psalm 130).

Shylock is spared the full force of the law, but he is obliged to convert – the feature of the play most unpalatable to modern audiences, Christians included. Perhaps Shakespeare too disliked it, one cannot tell. Is it likely that the playwright rose entirely above the context and belief of his time? Religious liberty was not yet an accepted ideal. All churches taught that conversion was necessary to salvation. Toleration, freedom of conscience in religion, was accepted only at the end of the wars of religion in north-west Europe, 50 years after *The Merchant*. A play written in one context is now received in another.

It can be said that Antonio, chastened by the ordeal he brought on himself for spitting on Shylock, finally behaves better, but Shakespeare does not show most Gentile behaviour as gentle. Readers have seen that the play refers often to biblical archetypes: the prodigal son, Jacob's tricks, a Daniel come to judgement. But non-biblical parallels are prominent also, often with stories from Ovid's *Metamorphoses*. The Venetian suitors compare themselves to Jason venturing for the Golden Fleece; and Shylock's daughter is like Medea tricking her father to help Jason. The tricks in this comedy have no divine sanction, and its comedy is not festive – unless one can rejoice not only in the escape of the prey but also in the outwitting of the predator – for the logic of the original folk tale is that Shylock's cruelty gets its just deserts. Shylock's 'pound of flesh' is still proverbial, and some in the audience would surely have rejoiced at the predator's humiliation as unthinkingly as

Gratiano does. The penalties imposed by the Duke, already reduced by Antonio's clemency, are complex, rapidly handed down, and not easily grasped. But when grasped they are designed to show Christian mercy as better than Shylock's vengeful justice, and perhaps than Judaic justice more generally. The play remains troubling, and not just for those who hate racism.

Understanding of context has led this chapter to dwell on religious references and virtues at the expense of another historical context, which might be termed the moral context of early capitalism. Much of the motivation of the action is competitive and mercantile. Family love is absent: Portia is a dutiful daughter to a dead father, but Jessica steals from her miserly father, squandering his money in a prodigal love-spree. Antonio forgives the prodigal Bassanio as a rich godfather might a godson; he is unreasonably generous. But life in Venice seems to be ruled by self-interest, except for Antonio and Portia, and (fleetingly at the trial) Bassanio. The generosity of Portia is not strained as she supports her husband's loyalty to his friend. At the end of the play Antonio stands alone, as sad as he was at the beginning. Isolation becomes a theme in Shakespeare's plays after Hal says to Falstaff, 'I know thee not, old man': it marks out Shylock, Jaques, Malvolio, Feste, the protagonists of the tragedies and many other characters, such as Pericles, Leontes, Hermione, Paulina, Antigonus, Prospero and Caliban.

The Merchant of Venice has been considered at length for several reasons: it is a play often misrepresented, partly because its original religious context can be overlooked. It raises in a painful form the question whether we should judge a work by attitudes likely to have prevailed at the time of composition or by those prevailing today, and whether these can be reconciled. This question arises differently elsewhere – in *Measure for Measure*, for example, or in *The Tempest*. The present discussion has been conducted in the belief that it is educative to try the historical path, to read the play as it stands, to 'direct' it oneself in the light of that understanding, partial as this must be. One educational value of the study of literature is the recognition that some of the values of a writer of the past are not those of the present. In 1939, W. H. Auden, on hearing of the death of a master with whose opinions he strongly disagreed, wrote in his 'In Memory of

W. B. Yeats' that the dead poet would soon 'be punished under a foreign code of conscience'.[7]

Shylock, finally, is the first example in Shakespeare of a character who can, as Yeats put it, 'engross the present and dominate memory' – both on the stage and in the play's reception – by virtue of the energy of his speech in a few scenes. This dominance has little to do with whether the character is admirable but whether it is more forceful or colourful than others. Falstaff, at about the same period of Shakespeare's career, has a similar effect, in three plays.

8
To the Globe

Much Ado About Nothing

Drama needs some conflict, and the conflict in *Much Ado About Nothing* can be uncomfortable, if not in the same way as in *The Merchant of Venice*. *Much Ado* lacks the poetry of most of Shakespeare's comedies of love, but it is an effective stage play, with a fine central role for Beatrice. The situation of a couple mutually attracted but each accustomed to dominate in conversation is ideal for the stage, and the play is well constructed. Yet the devices by which their friends – and Shakespeare – bring Beatrice and Benedick together are mechanical; their brilliant wit contests can now seem laboured; and the humour of Dogberry and his associates, though simple, is often unretrievable.[1] The play is predominantly in a 'realistic' prose undiversified by the music and other charms of verse that enrich *As You Like It* and *Twelfth Night*, Shakespeare's next love comedies. It is a theatrical convention that a servant flirting at her window might be mistaken for her mistress; but that Claudio could shame Hero in church on such a basis is grotesque. Claudio's shallowness allows Beatrice to make Benedick prove his seriousness; but audience discomfort remains. As in *The Merchant*, Shakespeare has taken an improbable story with powerful dramatic possibilities, but the deeper humanity he gives the flat characters of the original tale again deepens the difficulties caused by scenes such as the denunciation of a bride at the altar; her friend's dramatic demand that Benedick 'kill Claudio'; and the bride's apparent return from the dead. *Much Ado* is better to see than to read, and better to read than to think about.

In 1599, the Lord Chamberlain's Men moved their operations from north of London to south of the Thames, and moved the timbers of their Theatre to Bankside; the Theatre was now the Globe, an indication of its growing importance. The story is told in James Shapiro's *1599: A Year in the Life of William Shakespeare.*[2] The first play the company put on there was a political tragedy of a new kind.

Julius Caesar

Julius Caesar shows Shakespeare mastering tragedy as well as comedy and history. He had taken from ancient history the atrocities of *Titus Andronicus* and the dignified moral tableaux of *Lucrece*. He had given a tragic dimension to episodes in his English histories, some of which have 'tragedy' in their titles. Now he wrote a kind of play new to him, with apparent ease and with complete success. Julius Caesar, not Alexander, was the best-known commander of antiquity, and his murder was the standard example of an historical crime. This was an example also of the medieval idea of tragedy: the downfall of a great man. Dante put Brutus and Cassius in the lowest of the nine circles of his *Inferno*, clamped in the jaws of Satan, alongside Judas. To betray one's lord, whether Christ or Caesar, was to the medieval mind the vilest of sins. This view still held in monarchical England, though republican theorists justified tyrannicide, as did reformers such as John Knox (1513–72), and some Catholic thinkers.

Shakespeare's version of this oft-rehearsed story is largely taken from the *Lives of the Noble Grecians and Romans*, Sir Thomas North's lively translation of a French version made by Bishop

Jacques Amyot from the Greek of Plutarch: thus it was a four-stage process. Subjects of the Tudors naturally had an interest in the careers of the powerful, and Shakespeare adopted Plutarch's comparative approach to this hot topic. He made the story of the assassination of the most powerful of Western rulers into a play of unusual lucidity and rhetorical power, dwelling as much on what follows Caesar's death as on what led to it; at the end of the play we know Brutus better than Caesar. Brutus was descended from Lucius Junus Brutus, who, as reported in *Lucrece*, initiated the Republic, a republic that had lasted five centuries but was about to end. The noble Brutus is persuaded to act by the envious Cassius. The killing is presented as a very bloody murder, by several hands, and it happens in the Capitol, the centre of Rome; it sets off violent reactions, the deaths of innocents, and a civil war, and brings destruction to the conspirators. Motive and effect are clearly laid bare, so that there is less to explain in this play than in others by Shakespeare. Caesar's death comes quite early in the play. Brutus, not Caesar, is given the introspective soliloquies of Shakespeare's tragic protagonists. More generally characteristic of his way of conceiving a play is its dual focus, on Caesar and on Brutus. Dual focus makes for comparison and for divided sympathies. Richard II was a king bad enough to be deposed – and then a man badly treated. Here we learn to mistrust Caesar but also to mistrust Cassius. We see that blood will have blood, a theme of Senecan drama, but we also witness the effects of doing evil so that good may come, a Christian angle on a classical crime. Dual focus is found in many plays, and is in the titles of *Romeo and Juliet*, *Troilus and Cressida* and *Antony and Cleopatra*. Directing sympathy to and fro is basic to drama, as we have already seen in *The Merchant of Venice*.

Aristotle, who liked single focus in a tragedy, might still have liked this play. Its clarity of exposition and focus make it a convincing account of the political events it dramatises. Its language also has a steady intelligibility not always found in later tragedies, and it is a text which probably loses less in translation than any other Shakespeare play. 'Friends, Romans, countrymen', the speech which Brutus, 'an honourable man', allows Mark Antony to make, shows how oratory can turn a crowd into a mob. Caesar would have ruled as an autocrat, but his assassination leaves the stage to a demagogue. Shakespeare represents common people unusually well, while showing no respect for their collective political judgement. Modern Western audiences may feel a sympathy for Brutus that would have been less common in 1599. Stage history shows that political conditions, and audience predisposition, often determine the reception of plays in which rulers are killed. *Julius Caesar* would be a good play to see just before or just after the overthrow of a powerful ruler. The Essex rebellion of 1601 was the last of several attempts to overthrow Queen Elizabeth.

As You Like It

This is a comedy never seriously troubled by the dire outcomes threatened in *Much Ado About Nothing* or *The Merchant of Venice*. Drama needs an initial problem, a muddle in the middle, and a denouement: an untying of the knots. Tragedy ends in death, comedy knits up the ends in marital unions. *As You Like It* is as light and festive as its title suggests, yet it is an inventive play of some complexity, and characters count for less than the ideals they represent, and the dance of the story. Character interest is widely distributed.

Rosalind seems at first a heroine from theatrical stock. Good, loyal and oppressed, she falls in love at first sight; then runs away from a wicked court dressed as a man. So far, so romance. But she has an interesting personality – enterprising, realistic, spirited and intelligent. The wicked Duke Frederick has usurped the throne of Rosalind's father, Duke Senior, who lives a hard but virtuous exile in the Forest of Ardenne (the Belgian Ardennes, not the Warwickshire Arden). There, after some initial problems, and some songs and comic byplay, everything is resolved as we might 'like it' to be.

Characters in *As You Like It* come in pairs, good and bad: brother dukes whose blameless daughters, Rosalind and Celia, are closer than sisters; good and bad brothers, Orlando and Oliver. (Roland and Oliver were legendary comrades in the *Song of Roland*. Roland became Orlando in Ariosto's *Orlando Furioso*, which is where Shakespeare found the name.) Shakespeare's Orlando is, for no reason at all, hated by his brother, as Oliver helpfully explains: 'My soul, yet I know not why, hates nothing more than he. Yet he's gentle.' Antonio, the merchant of Venice, likewise did not know why he was so sad: he had a 'want-wit sadness'. As in the folk or fairy tales and the Romance tradition from which Shakespeare took his comedies, characters can be good or evil for no reason at all. Stage bastards are generally evil, stage daughters good.

In *As You Like It* things fall out as we would like them to. Orlando defeats the professional wrestler whom Oliver has set up to kill him; Rosalind falls for Orlando. Duke Frederick banishes Rosalind; she and Celia dress up as men and run away to the Forest, the scene of the rest of the action. Orlando's faithful old servant, Adam, is saved from death; Orlando saves Oliver from a lion; Oliver repents and reforms; Frederick gives the throne back to Duke Senior; and four couples are to wed. The action is full of disguise, coincidence and inventive complication. Celia and Rosalind dress as young men but call themselves Aliena and Ganymede, names suggesting role-play (Ganymede was Zeus's girlishly attractive cupbearer; Aliena means 'strange girl'). Ganymede then coaches Orlando in how he might woo Rosalind; thus Rosalind plays Ganymede playing the part of Rosalind. Orlando does not see through the disguise. There is also broad comedy with Touchstone, Audrey and a simple native of the forest of Ardenne called William.

The old servant Adam is ideally loyal, as Kent is in *King Lear*. Adam in the Book of Genesis has two sons, one of whom killed the other – as Oliver tries to kill Orlando here. Biblical parallels, analogies and allusions abound: to the prodigal son, to trees bringing forth good fruit, to the Ark, to a second flood, to damnation (though for 'lack of court manners'). The play is a parable with the moral messages of pastoral: rural hospitality is kinder than that of the court; 'sweet are the uses of adversity'. Pastoral is a sophisticated kind of literature, set in a country populated by shepherds and shepherdesses. There are minor stock characters from the world of classical pastoral: old Corin, and young Silvius, a shepherd, in love with Phoebe, a cold girl who will have none of him. She pursues Ganymede.

As You Like It, then, is a genre play. The advantage of genre is that the audience – which includes the reader – knows the conventions. (But pastoral has become an unfamiliar literary genre; it is not a game which people any longer play.) Names such as Orlando and Ganymede signal a literary world of legend and romance, in which banished noblemen break into song; in which woods are populated by philosophisers like the melancholy Jaques, a satirist of the pastoral life. Country wisdom trumps court smartness: the old shepherd Corin asks 'Who calls?' The court Fool, Touchstone, replies: 'Your betters, sir.' Corin: 'Else are they very wretched' (2.4.64–6). The play is literary, playful, witty: the main story is doubled or reflected upside down in subplots. Rosalind and Orlando are lovers paralleled by Sylvius and Phoebe, and Touchstone and Audrey. Sylvius and Phoebe use verse; Touchstone and Audrey, a country wench, use prose. Orlando uses verse to woo; hearing this, Jaques leaves the stage, exclaiming 'God buy you [Goodbye to you] if you talk in blank verse' (4.1.29). Verse in tragedy is for the nobility, but in this comedy prose is sense and love poems nonsense. 'Men have died from time to time,' Rosalind tells Orlando, 'and worms have ate them, but not for love' (4.1.94): disappointment in love is not fatal. Jaques and Touchstone are commentators who stand outside the action, and by pointing at its artifice make artifice acceptable. Touchstone notes that courtiers perfume themselves with the product of the perineal gland of a cat. (A touchstone was a tool used by assayers to tell true gold from fool's gold.) The forest of Ardenne, unlike most forests, is full of paradox and of philosophy: 'there's no clock in the forest' and 'all the world's a stage'.

The plot is a dance of familiar ideas, simple and sophisticated. The most artificial of theatre conventions is that when a girl disguises herself as a boy, no one except the audience can tell that this he is a she; even when it falls in love with a man who is in love with her. Such love disguise and cross-dressing take to extremes the artificiality of theatre, in which dress, acting, appearance and words can succeed only by the audience's make-believe. On Shakespeare's stage all female parts were played by boy actors, partly for the reason suggested by Noel Coward's song advising Mrs Worthington not to put her daughter on the stage: in case, as Celia says to Rosalind at 3.2.190, she 'put a man in her belly'. The Elizabethans lived much closer to the farmyard than we do. Is this how the daughters of Elizabethan dukes talked to each other?[3] Or is it Aliena speaking to Ganymede? Or one boy actor to another? For men to dress as women was normally forbidden – for one of the reasons that made it a rule in the theatre.[4]

In Shakespeare these confusions are usually innocent illusion, part of theatrical play. Since all acting is impersonation, the audience, knowing that Rosalind is played by a boy, treats her for the imaginative purposes of the play as a girl. But Shakespeare makes this girl dress as a boy, the sex of the actor. He then has this 'boy' play the part of Orlando's girl, inviting Orlando to practise his wooing on her. Amorous confusion is carried to lengths which make it laughable, intriguing, even thought provoking.

Disguise and role-play enables Ganymede to say to Orlando, 'I am your Rosalind' (4.1.58): Ganymede is Rosalind, a real woman as well as the addressee of Orlando's bad verse. In Act 5, Rosalind's game allows four lovers each to say in turn 'And I for no woman'. Such comedy is close to musical comedy and to opera. The songs in this play, such as 'Under the greenwood tree / Who loves to lie with me' (2.5) and 'It was a lover and his lass' (5.3) are fine examples of an essential element in Shakespearian comedy, an element growing in importance. This is the first time that Shakespeare uses a divinity on stage: Hymen, goddess of marriage, descends to restore a daughter to her father.

Twelfth Night

Twelfth Night, probably 1601, a comedy at least the equal of *As You Like It*, is taken next, before *Hamlet*, which was probably composed in 1600. Most of the poems in *Shake-speares Sonnets*, published in 1609, were written by this time. It is convenient to look at the Sonnets after *Twelfth Night* and before *Hamlet*, since *Hamlet* inaugurates the sequence of tragedies which dominates the third quarter of Shakespeare's writing career.

Twelfth Night is a ripe love comedy with a happy ending. Shipwrecked separately on the coast of Illyria are twins, Viola and Sebastian, each thinking the other drowned; each ends up marrying well. As in most Shakespeare plays about love, the pivot of the play is a girl, Viola. She disguises herself as a boy (Cesario), initally to evade detection rather than, like some heroines, to pursue a young man. Cesario (Viola) is employed by the young Duke Orsino to carry his love to the young Olivia. Both Olivia and Viola mourn a brother. But Olivia falls for Cesario and Viola/ Cesario falls in love with Orsino.

Orsino's opening words had announced the theme of longing:

> If music be the food of love, play on,
> Give me excess of it that, surfeiting
> The appetite may sicken and so die.
> That strain again, it had a dying fall.
> O, it came o'er my ear like the sweet sound
> That breathes upon a bank of violets,
> Stealing and giving odour. Enough, no more,
> 'Tis not so sweet now as it was before.

(1.1.1–8)

This play is as much music as action: the players dance to a series of variations upon love. Orsino and Olivia swoon affectedly in their love-sickness. When Orsino says that women's hearts lack retention, Viola disagrees:

> My father had a daughter loved a man
> As it might be, perhaps, were I a woman
> I should your lordship.
> *Orsino*: And what's her history?
> *Viola*: A blank, my lord. She never told her love ...

(2.4.106–9)

The dramatic irony here is pleasantly shared between Viola and the audience. Viola's love is discreet, patient, unpossessive, undisclosed. Beneath the smoothly plangent strings there is a scherzo of wind instruments led by Sir Toby Belch, who sits up late guzzling the cakes and ale of his niece Olivia, and singing loud catches, to the disgust of the puritan Malvolio, Olivia's steward. Malvolio, as his name suggests, is 'sick of self-love'. He is tricked by a forged letter written by another servant, Maria, into thinking that his mistress wants him to woo her. In a very funny scene, Malvolio's declarations convince Olivia he is mad. Olivia is then tricked into marrying Viola's lost twin Sebastian. Viola reveals herself to Sebastian, Maria marries the undeserving Toby, and Viola her wonderful Orsino. The humiliated Malvolio is unmated; so too is the clown Feste, who sings the songs, 'O Mistress mine, where are you roaming?', 'Come away, come away death' and 'When that

I was and a little tiny boy'. The songs lend a background nostalgia to the amorous games of this baroquely musical play, written by a man of 37, middle-aged for an Elizabethan. *Twelfth Night*, the last day of Christmas and a good day to put a spoilsport in a cellar, is the end of the festive season.

Feste is one of Shakespeare's best fools. Henry VIII and James I kept licensed fools, and the popes kept one until the eighteenth century. Shakespeare develops the jester into a choric figure. His fools joke and sing, and make fun of their betters – as, though more discreetly, did the Lord Chamberlain's Men. Feste's songs are sad, and there is a balance in *Twelfth Night* between those things which make romance and fairy tale – lucky meetings, discoveries, recognitions, the promise of love fulfilled, the restoration of a lost twin – and a sense of a time-governed world in which these wished-for things do not happen.

Viola and Sebastian are brother and sister twins. It is hard to forget that Shakespeare was the father of such twins, of whom the boy died, aged 11. This is not to say that he writes autobiographically, for most of his plays show a great interest in doubling and identity, an interest which might occur to a thinking man of the theatre who did not have twins.

Sexual envy and possessiveness are themes of *A Midsummer Night's Dream* and *Much Ado*, and become more insistent in the so-called 'problem plays' and in the Sonnets, and in *Hamlet*, *King Lear* and *Antony and Cleopatra*. Jealousy is the subject of *Othello* and of half of *The Winter's Tale*. Among the many variations of love explored in *Twelfth Night* jealousy never becomes a disturbing force. Although highly sophisticated and far from blithe, it is the last of Shakespeare's plays that might be called innocent. Some years later he was to return to the theme of innocence and youth.

Shake-speares Sonnets

Although this volume was not published until 1609, Francis Meres mentions Shakespeare sonnets in circulation by 1598. It is thought that most of the sonnets were composed by then, and all of them by 1604; this therefore is the right chronological point at which to discuss them. It is not known whether we have anything written by Shakespeare before he was 26 or 27, though one sonnet seems early: the weak sonnet 145, addressed to Anne Hathaway. Shakespeare's contemporaries called him 'poet'; recorded English does not show the words 'playwright' and 'dramatist' until 1616 and 1660 respectively.[5] By 1594 Shakespeare was a poet in the modern sense of the word, admired for his *Venus and Adonis* and *Lucrece*, though these are poems so unlike most modern poems as to be an acquired taste.

For two centuries readers have thought that the best of Shakespeare's 'non-dramatic' poems is to be found in a volume entitled *Shake-speares Sonnets*, published in 1609 but begun at the same time as the other poems grouped together as non-dramatic. 'Non-dramatic' is a term coined to distinguish the narrative poems, the Sonnets and 'The Phoenix and the Turtle' from the stage plays. The 1623 Folio, edited by theatre colleagues, collected the theatre work, not the poems. But 'non-dramatic' does not mean 'undramatic': the narrative poems are tableaux in a design laid out by a dramatist, and the Sonnets form a sequence which becomes dramatic. This can surprise modern readers of the Sonnets, who are used to reading single poems, not long sequences. Shakespeare's sonnets are often first sampled in very small numbers, often in anthologies that are largely lyrical. Lyric poems since Wordsworth have tended to be autobiographical or personal. The realisation that there are 154 of these highly artificial poems, in a sequence which has to be read as a whole, can be daunting. Also, reading through them eventually brings a realisation that the sequence cannot be simply autobiographical, so artificial is its narrative arrangement. It may not even be the case that Shakespeare is more autobiographical in the Sonnets than he is in his plays. His use of the personal pronoun 'I' does not mean he is writing about himself, even when, as in the opening of Sonnet 29, he persuades us that he is: 'When in disgrace with Fortune and men's eyes, / I all alone beweep my outcast state.'

The sonnet (from Italian *sonnetto*, little sound) is a verse form of (classically) 14 lines which are divided by their rhyme scheme into eight and six, usually with a switch of tack in the second half. It is found in Italy before the time of Dante, who used it. But a European fashion for the sonnet sequence was created by the fourteenth-century Tuscan poet Petrarch, whose *Canzoniere* has 317 sonnets in a narrative/dramatic sequence about his love for Laura, mostly love complaint in the first person. The sonnet carried medieval love lore into modern European poetry; the first sonnet in English is found in Chaucer's *Troilus and Criseyde*, and sonnets are love tokens in several of Shakespeare's comedies. Shakespeare was therefore following the example of other Elizabethan sonneteers, especially Sidney, in linking love sonnets into a sequence. Francis Meres says that the poet had allowed some of his 'sugared sonnets' to circulate 'among his private friends'. Their publication in 1609, ten years after the fashion for sonnets, is seemingly unauthorised, though perhaps not against the author's will. The book's cryptic dedication page has given rise to much inconclusive speculation. Whatever the facts behind the publication, the title *Shake-speares Sonnets* shows the commercial value of the author's name. Most sonnet sequences took their titles from a fictional beloved with a name such as Stella or Delia. The three beloveds who appear in this sonnet sequence are anonymous. The name of Shakespeare was the book's selling point.

Secrecy was part of the convention of sonneteering, and much in this unconventional sequence is not transparent. Yet in its dramatic fashion it projects a story that is intelligible, if at times opaque. There are 126 sonnets to a fine young nobleman, followed by 26 to a dark woman. The love poems to the young lord at first formally beg him to have children so that his beauty will not die. The voice of the poet then protests that the lovely boy's beauty will not die since these poems will keep him alive until the end of time. The love then grows more intensely emotional in its expression, as in Sonnets 29 and 30, but the youth's physical beauty, it gradually emerges, is not matched by any moral beauty. The poet's love is ideal and unselfish, but the addressee exploits the devastating effect of his looks and his rank. The poet attempts to believe the best, but unease grows and finally breaks out in disgust: 'Lilies that fester smell far worse than weeds' (Sonnet 94). In the 12 lines of the deliberately incomplete sonnet 126, the poet drops his claim that poetry will preserve youthful beauty – and unselfish love – against Time and death.

It is a surprise for modern readers to discover that most of the Sonnets trace the story of an ideal love for a fine-looking noble youth. The relationship is a unique variant on a Renaissance tradition of noble male friendship. For sonnet readers in 1609 it would probably have been more of a surprise to discover, late in the sequence, that this loving poet has a mistress – of the 'wrong' sort: not fair, young and noble, not chaste, not admirable. His love for the 'woman coloured ill', known to posterity as 'the Dark Lady', is explicitly sexual, obsessively so, and she is free with her sexual favours, making her 'a bay where all men ride'. Though dark, she is not, in most senses of the word, a lady. Such carnal and conflicted relationships can be found in classical Latin poetry, but not in Petrarchan tradition. The poet's illicit relationship with her calls for mutual pretences of love. At the crisis the poet abandons poetic enrichment and obliquity for a painfully plain confession: 'Two loves I have, of comfort and despair' (Sonnet 144): the poet's fair youth and dark woman come together in a sexual union which doubly betrays the poet. The sequence ends in humiliated revulsion, and is followed by two frigid epigrams on the burns inflicted by Cupid. Then follows a stanzaic narrative of 329 lines, *A Lover's Complaint*, which most now accept as Shakespeare's own conclusion to the sequence. In it, a shepherdess complains of being seduced and abandoned by a young man of extraordinary beauty and eloquence. This anti-idyll clarifies the design and the theme of the preceding sonnets, for the lover complained of is to be identified with the château-bottled seducer of Sonnets 1–126, as experienced by one of his victims. She ends by confessing that if he wooed her again he 'Would yet again betray the fore-betrayed': she would fall again, knowing that she would again be abandoned.

The volume has, then, four main characters – the poet of all 154 sonnets, the ruined maid of *A Lover's Complaint*, the fair youth and the dark woman – but two speaking parts, the poet and the ruined maid. The sequence dramatises love unsatisfied. Neither of the poet's loves can be truly satisfied: that for the young man cannot be physically satisfied, simply because he is a man, as is made explicitly clear in Sonnet 20; that for the woman cannot be lastingly satisfied, because it is lust. *A Lover's Complaint* shows the delusive and predatory sides of sexual love and desire (just as in Shakespeare's two narrative poems). *A Lover's Complaint* completes the sequence so schematically as to disable a simple biographical reading of these poems. Neither of the poet's loves has the normal outcome of sexual love, the procreation of children. This fits well with the insistent advice to 'breed' with which the sequence opens: 'From fairest creatures we desire increase'. But there is no increase, no child, only an expanding sense of waste, an expansion which can be represented formally: A loves B ideally. A loves C sexually. B and C love sexually. A is left out. A hears D complain that she has been seduced by B, and would willingly be seduced again.

Shake-speares Sonnets is a baffling volume, and at first the sequence seems less than the sum of its parts. The parts vary in interest and quality, but a design emerges through reading and the sense of the sequence can be made out. The Sonnets imply, though only eventually, a story both complex and unhappy. This surprises those who know only the anthology pieces, such as love's sensuous appeal in 'Shall I compare thee to a summer's day' (18); the noble sentiments of 'Let me not to the marriage of true minds' (116); the emotion of 'When to the sessions of sweet silent thought' (30); the grandeur of 'Like as the waves make toward the pebbled shore' (60); and the melancholy of Sonnet 73 here:

> That time of year thou mayst in me behold
> When yellow leaves or none or few do hang
> Upon those boughs which shake against the cold,
> Bare ruined choirs where late the sweet birds sang.

The lavish appeal of such poems is not to be denied; compared with other sonneteers, Shakespeare writes a mightier line in a simpler rhyme scheme, affording a more dramatic delivery. The sonnet is a highly artificial form, with its own conventions, some of which Shakespeare turns to radically new uses. But the style is consistently rich and complex, the diction and movement of the verse often majestic, and the sense often tortuous or veiled, or both. The Scottish poet Hugh MacDiarmid isolated a line in Sonnet 107 as a line both typical of Shakespeare, and one which could not be written by a Scotsman: 'And peace proclaims olives of endless age.' But these excessively beautiful poems, taken together, are rich not only in art and expression, but also in dramatic intelligence. Their generous idealism is gradually penetrated by an understanding of love's illusions.

Sonnet 73 ends: 'This thou perceiv'st, which makes thy love more strong / To love that well which thou must leave ere long.' This compliments the young man for continuing to cherish the ageing poet. But this courteous acknowledgement of inequalities in age, social rank and intensity of love also recognises that the young man's kind attention will not last. The end conceals a reproach: 'well' may be a play on the poet's name, Will. (Two later sonnets are entirely devoted to obsessive plays on 'Will' as Desire.) Such cryptic signatures encourage us, if we need encouragement, to take the 'I', the writer/speaker, as Shakespeare himself; yet the detectives identifying the poet's loves and the rival poet are all in the dark, pinning fictional tails on biographical donkeys. The Sonnets move between the poles of autobiography and Sidneian romance. Although Shakespeare often sounds as if he is speaking openly, the relationships in the Sonnets are always dramatised. 'Will' names himself and itself but does not name his rival loves. Their real or fictional identities remain cryptic, as does the sequence itself. This cryptic quality is a major difference between a sonnet sequence and the explicitness of a play for the public stage.

There is one area in which the dramatised voice may be personal. 'Shall I compare thee to a summer's day' ends: 'So long as men can breathe and eyes can see / So long lives this and this gives life to thee.' The claim is that this poem will live to the end of time, or for as long as men read English verse aloud. This brag, though made in a love poem, may be Shakespeare's own. Yet the claim has to be surrendered. The poet concedes in 126 that the 'lovely boy' must be rendered by Nature to Time, the enemy of human love. Two Christian sonnets, 55 and 146, look beyond death and beyond Doomsday, but the series, like erotic poetry in general, is this-worldly. *Shake-speares Sonnets* contains some of our finest love poems, but the note is not very often that of 'the lark at break of day arising'. In the end, the sequence dramatises the misery of love in this world as much as, or more than, its splendours.

9
Horatio's Question

The Tragedy of Hamlet, Prince of Denmark, the most varied, complex and exciting of Shakespeare's plays, seems to have been a hit. It travelled far from the boards of the Globe. Two different printed versions soon appeared, and English players took the play to Germany. *Hamlet* is revived more often than any other play, reappearing on the stages and in the literatures of the world. Generations have read, performed, watched and quoted from *Hamlet*. Indeed the play has become so familiar in the English-speaking world that its reappearances in later literature are not always serious, as for example in Mr Wopsle's comically inept performance in *Great Expectations*. In foreign literature it retains its tragic status. The poet Boris Pasternak, who translated several Shakespeare plays into Russian, ends his novel *Dr Zhivago* with the poems of his protagonist, the first of which is 'Hamlet', which in the English translation of 1958 begins, 'The noise is stilled. I come out on to the stage'.[1] Hamlet's 'To be or not to be' also inhabits other languages. The French know that Hamlet pondered the question *Être ou ne pas être*. Italian newspapers used to refer to Pope Paul VI, a scrupulous and cautious pontiff, much exercised by intractable problems, as *troppo amletico*.

Hamlet survives in three different texts, a problem for textual editors. The origins and interpretation of the play raise other problems. Some editors compound this by preserving every puzzle that has arisen in connection with the play and treating all as important. There is no need to join in this game. Thus, in Act 1 Hamlet thinks of 'going back to school at Wittenberg', yet in Act 5 recalls that as a child he was carried on the back of a man who has been dead for 23 years. Is Hamlet in his teens or his late twenties? The latter is more likely, but the inconsistency matters less than it would in a detective story. New readers are strongly advised to read through the text at one sitting, from 'Who's there?' on the ramparts at Elsinore through to the last line: 'Go, bid the soldiers shoot.' After having read the play, they may wonder at problems it directly raises, such as Hamlet's treatment of Ophelia. It is worth quoting the similar advice Samuel Johnson offers readers towards the end of his *Preface to Shakespeare*: 'Notes are often necessary, but they are necessary evils. Let him that is yet unacquainted with the powers of Shakespeare, and who desired to feel the highest pleasure that the drama can give, read every play from the first scene to the last, with utter negligence of all his commentators.'[2]

Something needs to be said of the three texts of *Hamlet*. The first Quarto (Q1, 1603) has about 2200 lines; the second Quarto (Q2, 1604/5) has about 3800 lines. Q2 is the basis of the Folio text (F1, 1623), which is 230 lines shorter and has other differences. The title page of Q1 claims to give it 'as it hath been acted' (Illustration 7). It is an imperfect text, perhaps worked up into print from an actor's memory of performances, probably to get a popular play out of the clutches of its owners, the King's Men. The title page of Q2 reads: 'Newly imprinted and enlarged to almost as much againe as it was, according to the true and perfect Coppie' (Illustration 8). The longer versions read much better, and are too long for the stage. Many editors take F1 as their base text; some prefer Q2. All these editors take some readings from both the other texts, to make a composite or eclectic text, an ideal or best text. Some recent editors say there is no text of *Hamlet*, only texts – and print all three. This is defensible as scholarship but of little help to readers and actors. Theatres continue to use cut-down versions of the composite texts found in the older editions.

Hamlet has a mythical status. Indeed, its reputation preceded it, for it built on an earlier Hamlet play, now lost. In 1589 Thomas Nashe wrote that 'English Seneca read by candlelight yields many good sentences as "Blood is a beggar", and so forth: an if you intreat him fair in a frosty morning, he will afford you whole Hamlets, I should say handfuls of tragical speeches.'[3] Nashe's smart remark reminds us that plays in English were read in private

THE
Tragicall Hiſtorie of
HAMLET
Prince of Denmarke

By William Shake-ſpeare.

As it hath beene diuerſe times acted by his Highneſſe ſer-
uants in the Cittie of London : as alſo in the two V-
niuerſities of Cambridge and Oxford, and elſe-where

At London printed for N.L. and Iohn Trundell.
1603.

Illustration 7 The title page of Quarto 1 of *Hamlet*, 'as it hath been acted',
1603. See discussion on page 101. In Q1, 'To be or not to be' is followed
by 'I there's the point, / To Die, to sleepe, to dream, I mary there it goes.'
By permission of the Folger Shakespeare Library

THE

Tragicall Hiſtorie of

H A M L E T,

Prince of Denmarke.

By William Shakeſpeare.

Newly imprinted and enlarged to almoſt as much
againe as it was, according to the true and perfeᵗ
Coppie.

AT LONDON,
Printed by I. R. for N. L. and are to be ſold at his
ſhoppe vnder Saint Dunſtons Church in
Fleetſtreet. 1 6 o 4.

Illustration 8 The title page of Quarto 2 of *Hamlet*, 'enlarged to almost as
much again as it was' (i.e., in Q1), 'according to the true and perfect copie'
(unlike Q1), 1604. See page 101. By permission of the Folger Shakespeare
Library

before Shakespeare was well into his writing career. It also tells us that this first *Hamlet* featured 'handfuls of tragical speeches' and 'good sentences'; the *Hamlet* Shakespeare composed about 1600 has both of these. Its tragic soliloquies are famous and its good sentences have passed into the language. 'I liked the play but had not realised it was so full of quotations' is one of those 'overheard' thoughts attributed to other people. But the remark is less silly than it seems, for *Hamlet* is indeed full of good sentences, nuggets, quotable moral sayings of a proverbial kind, ideas not original to Shakespeare but given a good turn in his words (poetry is written with words, not ideas).

The irreverent Nashe is not the only person to refer to an ear-lier Hamlet play famous in 1589. This was when Shakespeare was doing his first playwriting, often in collaboration with others. This *Ur-Hamlet*, probably by Kyd, had a Ghost who cried 'Hamlet, Revenge!' Seneca's ghosts demanding revenge, and mad avengers, both appeared in Kyd's *Spanish Tragedy* of *c*.1587, a bloodthirsty, flesh-creeping hit which started a stage tradition which Shakespeare's *Hamlet* parodies and transforms. The early play came from the story of Amleth, which features in a legendary history of the Danish throne, known to Shakespeare through a French collec-tion of tragic stories. To his sources, Shakespeare added variety, humour and pathos in the episodes of the players and their play, Ophelia's madness and death, the gravediggers, Ophelia's funeral and much else – including the character of Hamlet.

Horatio obeys the dying Prince's request that he should live long enough 'to tell my story'. Horatio's report can also serve as the recipe for the genre of revenge tragedy:

> you shall hear
> Of carnal, bloody, and unnatural acts,
> Of accidental judgements, casual slaughters,
> Of deaths put on by cunning and forced cause;
> And, in this upshot, purposes mistook
> Fallen on th'inventors' heads.
>
> (5.2.385–90)

Nashe's phrase 'English Seneca' indicates a kind of tragedy which was read privately by candlelight as well as performed on stages.

It showed a world corrupt, malignant, mad and corpse-strewn; its incident and language are sensational. This craze for Senecan *noir* lasted from the 1580s to the 1620s. Though *Hamlet* certainly has these ingredients, it has others which will have puzzled revenge tragedy addicts – rather as the loves shown in *Shake-speares Sonnets* are not those familiar from older sonnet sequences. For its revenger is not a man of action like Laertes and Fortinbras but a man of words: he confesses in six long soliloquies that he is not comfortable in the role assigned to him. The obligation to revenge is a special instance of the tragic plight required in a tragedy: a good man in a bad situation from which there is no good way out. 'The time is out of joint,' says Hamlet, closing Act 1: 'O cursed spite! / That ever I was born to set it right.'

When Hamlet acts madly, the distraught Ophelia speaks of his qualities in lines which show Shakespeare's verse at its most formally memorable:

> O what a noble mind is here o'erthrown!
> The courtier's, soldier's, scholar's eye, tongue, sword,
> Th' expectancy and rose of the fair state,
> The glass of fashion and the mould of form.

> (3.1.151–4)

Earlier, Hamlet's own 'What a piece of work is a man!' (2.2.303) is consonant with Ophelia's tribute, and confirms that he appreciated those humanist ideals. Yet it concludes, 'Man delights not me.' Hamlet's state of mind is understandable. 'The observed of all observers', he is kept at court under the eye of his loathed uncle. Succession in medieval Denmark, as in medieval Scotland, was elective: the rule of male primogeniture was not established. Yet we can assume that Hamlet would have been chosen as king had his mother not married his uncle. Hamlet, as it turns out, was not born to rule, but the Ghost's command constrains him to set right the frame of this disjointed time. Hamlet ponders, tests out the Ghost's word and the King's guilt, outwits his watchers and reproaches his mother, but delays. Revenge tragedy was about action, and action deferred increases suspense, which is one reason why the play's grip on us never relaxes. Only when Hamlet is sent to England to be killed can he move to defend himself, which he does with startling ruthlessness. He accepts the duel proposed by his uncle with calm relief, knowing that Claudius is setting a trap of some kind. The action so long suspended now begins: the cards fall, the plot unwinds, the bodies fall, the last words are said. The last scene of *Hamlet* can produce a strange satisfaction, a quasi-aesthetic reaction peculiar to tragic endings. If such things must be, this is how they ought to happen. The mood is set by Hamlet's 'There is a special providence in the fall of a sparrow. If it be now, 'tis not to come; it if be not to come, it will be now; if it be not now, yet it will come. The readiness is all' (5.2.215–18).

The reader may not share this reaction, which is connected to an idea of tragedy older than the revenge play. Immediately after the death of the protagonist, at the climax of the first great tragedy in English, Horatio, Hamlet's philosophical friend, asks a philosophical question about tragedy. Horatio's question – 'What is it you would see?' – is directed to Fortinbras on the stage, but also directed from the stage to the audience: 'What is it you would see? / If ought of woe or wonder, cease your search' (5.2.367–8). On the stage we see a 'quarry': a squared-up pile of freshly killed bodies, collected at the end of a day's hunting. The bodies are those of the king, the queen, the prince, and the son of the late chief minister. A sight of woe and wonder, certainly, for young Fortinbras, who has Hamlet's 'dying voice' [his vote] to become the next king of Denmark. Horatio's question also asks the audience what it has come to see: what it expects from a tragedy. This is the question which Aristotle sought systematically to answer in his lectures on drama known as the *Poetics*.

'Woe or wonder' is Shakespeare's version of the emotions which, according to the findings of Aristotle, tragedy can induce in an audience: pain at another's undeserved suffering; awe at the realisation that this could happen to one's self. Modern discussion of tragedy descends from Aristotle, and discussion of drama takes much of its terminology from Greek – protagonist, character, climax, tragic irony, catastrophe, to name a few. A student of Shakespeare's tragedy should look at the *Poetics*, though it survives only in condensed note-form. In it we read that tragedy ideally has one protagonist, noble in rank and nature, yet not so noble that we cannot identify with him or her. The protagonist's tragic situation is followed by an *agon* or ordeal. *Hubris*, overweening pride, will provoke *nemesis*, fate, and a chain of consequences. Shakespeare may not have known these terms, or terms such as *anagnorisis*, recognition, or *peripeteia*, reversal; but he does the things to which the terms refer. He seems to know of Aristotle's view of the emotions induced in the audience by the tragic catastrophe. He knew of Sir Philip Sidney's *Defence of Poesy* (1579), which gives these emotions the Latinate names of 'commiseration' (compassion) and 'admiration' (awe). Modern translators usually choose 'pity' and 'fear'. Aristotle, whose scientific interests included biology, uses a physical analogy in concluding that this pity and fear induced *catharsis*, a purging or cleansing of the psyche of the audience. He found that the best Greek tragedies kept a single focus and unity of action. This diagnosis was erected by humanist theorists into a prescription: true tragedy observes unity in action, place and time, so that everything should happen in the same place on a single day; some theorists added, in three hours of real time (this condition is met in Shakespeare's last solo work, *The Tempest*). Of the four major tragedies, two keep a single focus, *Macbeth* and *Othello*. *King Lear* has a secondary storyline, derived from Sidney's *Arcadia*. In *Hamlet*, the Prince is the focus – when he is offstage, those onstage talk about him – but the plot is complex, and some of the Scandinavian military history is hard to take in. Shakespeare's practice in tragedy borrowed initially from Seneca, Kyd and Marlowe, but *Hamlet* goes far beyond the limited scope of the revenge tragedy, and invokes older and grander ideas of tragedy. In *Hamlet*, and in the tragedies that follow it, he also made skilful use of the jocularity found in Kyd and older English drama.

Education in Shakespeare's day was rhetorical, and genres had known conventions. Polonius says of the players that they are 'The best actors in the world, either for tragedy, comedy, history; pastoral, pastoral-comical, historical-pastoral, tragical-historical-pastoral, comical-historical-pastoral, scene individible, or poem unlimited.' This crescendo of pedantry soon becomes comical, but the ears of pedants in the audience may have noticed that Polonius's list of classifications develops in the direction of the play they were at. *Hamlet* is 'tragical-historical-comical' and may be 'scene individible' and 'poem unlimited'. Shakespeare was not ruled by theory, but he knew how to use generic expectation and how to go against it.

Rhetorical decorum has some slight bearing on the question of whether we are to admire Hamlet. Consider his opening words:

Claudius: But now my cousin Hamlet, and my son –
Hamlet: A little more than kin, and less than kind.
Claudius: How is it that the clouds still hang on you?
Hamlet: Not so, my lord, I am too much i' th' sun.

(1.2.64–7)

Hamlet's first line is a sour play on words, his second a bitter pun. If there are such jokes in classical tragedy we do not hear them. Neoclassical critics objected to Hamlet's twisting of the language as another sign of Shakespeare's 'barbarity'. We post-Romantics appreciate Hamlet's rejoinders because we sympathise with his impossible situation.

Is he, however, to be admired? Ophelia and his mother admired him. He has courage, brains and other qualities: he braves the Ghost, stands his ground against his uncle, sees through and mocks Polonius, Rosencrantz and Guildenstern, and wins the admiration of the dying Laertes. He speaks well, though his eloquence is really Shakespeare's. But however well he speaks, his conduct deteriorates and our view changes with his treatment of Ophelia, the bait in her father's trap. Idolising his own father, he is fierce with Gertrude, who is innocent of her husband's murder. He kills in haste, and speaks brutally of the corpse; he spares Claudius in order that he may go to hell. He protests too much in Ophelia's grave. He had 'put on an antic disposition' (1.5.180) but the mask of madness grows on him. His mind reels. Shakespeare presents cruelty to a woman, or attacks on women in general, as a sign of derangement; Hamlet, Lear and Othello rave against women, as does Leontes in *The Winter's Tale*. In the final scenes, however, once he is openly challenged, Hamlet's mind clears and he acts as well as he speaks. The play nevertheless implies a critique of revenge tragedy, and of revenge.

Identification and sympathy are not the same as admiration and approval. We need to identify with the protagonist for a tragedy to work; no involvement, no catharsis. We identify also with others in the play, Ophelia especially. We sympathise more easily with Hamlet in his isolation because we know what he knows, his soliloquies giving us unprecedented access to his interior mind and feelings. That his mother has married his father's murderer is known only to him and to us, and goes some way to explain his wish 'not to be'. A wish not to breed may explain why he breaks with Ophelia, whom he had loved. But no explanation reduces *Hamlet* to simplicity. The magical memorability of its opening scenes and of its major characters, the scope of the themes it unfolds, the variety, grandeur and power of its language, and its terrible climax, put it among the greater works of mankind.

As this book looks at about half of Shakespeare's plays, a representative sample, we should pause after discussing *Hamlet*, a very large play indeed, and an achievement of a greater order than the comedies, histories and tragedies which precede it. The kinds of plays William Shakespeare now composed begin to change, as the list in the next chapter may suggest.

10
Taken to Extremes

Plays of the third quarter

1600–1	*Twelfth Night*
	Hamlet
1601–2	*Troilus and Cressida*
1603–4	*Measure for Measure*
1604	*Othello*
1605	*All's Well that Ends Well*
	Timon of Athens
1605–6	*King Lear*
1605–6	*Macbeth*
1606–7	*Antony and Cleopatra*
1607–8	*Pericles*
1607–8	*Coriolanus*

(Dates of composition are approximate.)

The Quarto editions of some single plays have the words 'comedy', 'history' or 'tragedy' in their titles. The title page of the Folio (please look at Illustration 2, p. 4) puts history between comedy and tragedy, and the Folio orders the plays by genre, not, as modern editions usually do, in chronological order of composition. The placing of the histories between the received classical genres reflects Shakespeare's less polarised practice. The simplification of genre had worked for him in his early plays, *The Comedy of*

Errors and *Titus Andronicus*, and also in the unclassical romance comedies, which invite smiles rather than laughter. Genre then weakens. History becomes less tragic in *Henry IV*, and comedy appears in tragedy: Juliet's Nurse complicates the tragic effect. Shakespeare began with genre, then reverted to the habit of native English tradition, in which plays did not have generic purity. But he also addressed insoluble and existential problems not raised in medieval drama, though foreshadowed in William Langland's *Piers Plowman* – problems which defy the simplification of genre.

Problem plays

'Comedy', 'history' and 'tragedy' are useful terms. They enable the simple generalisation that Shakespeare began mostly with comedy and history, came later to tragedy and returned to comedy. But for those studying Shakespeare's 39 surviving plays at closer range, three categories are not enough. Polonius over-classifies, but classification has its uses. The present book has already found it helpful to mention Senecan tragedy, revenge tragedy, the tragedy of blood, romance comedy and love comedy. Chronology offers further groupings: the later comedies are often called the 'late romances', a term preferable to the 'last plays', since although they were Shakespeare's last single-handed pieces, he collaborated on three further plays. During the nineteenth century a rough order of composition of Shakespeare's plays became clear enough for its stages to be made out. A new class was proposed in 1896, by Frederick Boas, who suggested that a group of plays beginning with *Hamlet* – namely *Troilus and Cressida*, *Measure for Measure* and *All's Well that Ends Well* – should be considered as 'problem plays', since they address social or sexual problems in a new analytic spirit. Boas had noticed something, and the recent drama of the Norwegian playwright Henrik Ibsen offered an analogy. While most plays address a problem of some sort, the moral conundrums which these plays address are not resolved by the weddings in which they end; their spirit is satirical, quibbling, baffling, rather than simply comical. Boas's 'problem plays' were all written between 1600 and 1605. The term Boas proposed has proved convenient, except in the case of *Hamlet*, which is a tragedy, not a play narrowly concerned with a social problem or issue. (It should be said that Shakespeare's problem plays, unlike those of Ibsen, are not realist in style, are sparing in moral righteousness, and do not point to solutions.) Shakespeare's problem plays address extreme situations of the kind which gave rise to the saying that hard cases make bad law.

Whether or not these are called problem plays, the years in which they appeared had problems. Shakespeare had lived 39 years a subject of Queen Elizabeth. The Earl of Essex's failed coup of 1601 did not remove the ageing queen. In March 1603, however, she died, and the long rule of Henry VIII's three children came to an end. Later in that year *Measure for Measure* was performed. By then the King of Scotland, a foreign country often regarded by its southern neighbour as violent and difficult, had come to 'mingle with the English epicures', as *Macbeth* puts it. Queen Elizabeth had put Mary Queen of Scots, the new king's mother, to death. James came from a different nation and dynasty to Elizabeth, and a different religion; Scotland had a Kirk with presbyters, not a Church with bishops. Each Tudor ruler since Henry VII had brought in radical religious change. Would James Stuart be accepted? To whom would he listen? What would his policies be at home and abroad? Public affairs were unpredictable. In the event, James brought in peace with Spain, but no other major change, though his Scottish favourites were resented. Bishops were retained. But on 5 November 1605 came the Gunpowder Plot, an attempt to blow up the King in Parliament, made by some desperate young Catholics who felt betrayed by James's failure to keep to his assurances of toleration. The government took the opportunity to link the plot to Jesuits, and cracked down hard on Catholics.

Shakespeare's plays make few significant allusions to political events. An exception, in *Henry V*, shows the risks in doing so. This patriotic play had in 1599 openly predicted Essex's success in Ireland as well as praising Queen Elizabeth. But Essex's military expedition to Ireland ended in manifest failure; his attempted coup against the Queen in 1601 led to his execution. Shakespeare returned to setting his plays abroad or in the past. James was more generous towards drama than Queen Elizabeth had been, making the Lord Chamberlain's Men into the King's Men. Shakespeare was now working for James.

Measure for Measure

Two plays early in James's reign were calculated to appeal to the new king's interests, *Measure for Measure* and *Macbeth*. *Measure for Measure* is a play interested in problems, or rather cases: difficult and extreme cases of a kind that appealed to King James's learning and curiosity. James's education under the humanist George Buchanan had accustomed him to take an interest in controversy and disputation. The king fancied himself as a problem solver, an intellectual, a moral philosopher, a detective, an inquisitor (of witches) and a casuist. A casuist is one who specialises in hard cases, test cases, moral and legal cases difficult to adjudge.

The play is a kind of test case, argument or trial, about how government should treat extramarital sexual activity. In Vienna, Claudio and his fiancée Juliet had delayed marriage for financial reasons, but he has made her pregnant. The case of Juliet and Claudio has a parallel in the engagement of Angelo and Mariana, with the important difference that Angelo has, also for financial reasons, broken it off. Under a harsh old law of Vienna the sin of fornication was (according to the play) deemed a crime, carrying the death penalty. The 'precise' (i.e., godly, puritanical) Angelo is placed in charge of the city by its Duke, who absents himself. The first act of the new governor is to sentence Claudio to death under this old law, intending this exemplary punishment as a deterrent in a city in which sexual licence has risen to dangerous heights. Claudio's sister, Isabella, is a religious postulant who regrets that the restraints of the convent of St Clare, which she is about to enter, hoping to become a nun, are not strict enough. (Austrian Vienna was a Catholic city and Isabella a Catholic name: the Archduchess Isabella, daughter of Philip II of Spain, once the husband of Mary Tudor, had become ruler of the Spanish Netherlands.) Isabella is asked by her brother to plead with Angelo for his life; but her appearance and her plea excite Angelo's lust. He makes an indecent proposal – 'you sleep with me and I'll let your brother off' – from which Isabella understandably recoils. At this point the Duke secretly returns, disguised as a friar, and fantastic devices take over a plot already focused on impossible choices and desperate remedies.

Justice and mercy are the larger themes of this play, with a specific focus on how to control the houses in which sex was for sale, then known as bawdy houses or the stews – from which, as the text makes clear, there spread a sexual disease new to Europe. Bawdy houses stood near to the Globe on Bankside, the south bank of the Thames; neither theatres nor bawdy houses were allowed by law within the City, just across the river. Some patrons of the Globe will also have patronised bawdy houses. An Elizabethan Poor Law had named players along with vagabonds and sturdy beggars as dangers to society. Shakespeare's company were now the King's Men, and players were becoming almost respectable. There were no King's Women.

Sex is an area where ideals and actualities can be very far apart, but some things can be suggested about the attitudes of that time. First, as a natural function in a world with little privacy, sex attracted less fuss. As is well known, sex leads to 'increase', a growth in the number of human beings in creation; hence the teaching that it should be confined to marriage. This church teaching, though often ignored, was not publicly questioned.

These generalisations bear on an exchange between Lucio, a 'light' gentleman, and the virginal postulant Isabella:

Lucio: Your brother and his lover have embraced.
           As those that feed grow full, as blossoming time
           That from the seedness the bare fallow brings
           To teeming foison, even so her plenteous womb
           Expresseth his full tilth and husbandry.

(1.4.40–4)

Lucio, a witty libertine, has been commissioned by Claudio to give Isabella the news. He dresses the pregnancy in epic clothing. By stage convention, messengers always speak in an elevated way, a rule inherited from classical drama, but Lucio's out-of-character speech makes this pregnancy shine like a good deed in the naughty world of the play. Lucio may or may not expect that a novice nun might have ambiguous feelings about such a pregnancy, but Isabella, a true Shakespeare comedy heroine, responds with no fuss: 'Someone with child by him? My cousin Juliet. / [...] O let him marry her.' Today, as in 1603, the conception of children can be a consequence of sexual intercourse, but the mass availability of contraception has since the 1960s made this consequence avoidable, and attitudes have changed. When Claudio speaks of 'our most mutual entertainment', the last of his words does not have its modern sense. Sexual intercourse could not safely be regarded as 'recreational'; besides, between unmarried people it was not only a sin but also a crime, an offence punishable by law. Cases were tried in the church courts, popularly known therefore as the bawdy courts. Not long before Shakespeare's death in 1616, Thomas Quiney, two weeks married to the poet's younger daughter Judith, was found guilty by Stratford's Church Court of 'incontinence' with another woman. This (married) woman had died in childbirth, as had the child, on the day before the court case. Quiney was sentenced to public penance in church for three Sundays, though he remitted this by paying a fine. (In 1786, the Scottish poet Robert Burns made public penance in precisely this way for 'ante-nuptial fornication'.)

The issues in *Measure for Measure* are serious, but a play is not real life, and the characters are not a case load of individuals, as pretended in a realist novel, film or typecast television drama. The plot of this play is not at all real. The 'fantastical Duke' leaves his deputy to clean up the licentiousness of Vienna, then returns disguised as a hooded friar. This false religious identity allows him to act as a confessor and spiritual director to his subjects, and he directs them like an onstage theatre director. The Duke arranges a 'bed-trick', whereby Angelo sleeps with his fiancée Mariana, thinking her to be Isabella. This, in law, completes the engagement they had contracted. Angelo fails to detect the substitution. (A similar deception in the Book of Genesis leads to Jacob having to marry Leah rather than her more beautiful sister.) Improving on this bed-trick, the Duke now arranges a 'head-trick'. Angelo goes back on his word to Isabella and orders that Claudio be beheaded immediately. The Duke forestalls this, arranging that a convicted criminal, conveniently very drunk, should be beheaded instead of Claudio. (A better drinker volunteers for a similar role at the end of Dickens's *A Tale of Two Cities*.) When Angelo's hypocrisy and treachery are revealed in the final scene he says: 'When I perceive your grace, like power divine, / Has looked upon my passes', then asks for instant execution (5.1.370). Mariana and Isabella kneel to beg forgiveness for Angelo. The Duke throws off his hood, resumes his authority, and, turning to Mariana, tells Angelo to 'marry her instantly'. He next turns to the novice Isabella, saying, perhaps with a ducal smile, 'give me your hand and say you will be mine' (5.1.490). The Duke had earlier tested Isabella by telling her, falsely, that her brother's 'head is off'. Isabella does not have the chance to express her happy acceptance of the honour done her by the Duke. Gasp! But it's only a play. And, if we are invited to think, it may not be about forgiveness, or the arrogance of privilege, or what is expected of women, but that Shakespeare is happy enough to leave us gasping.

The title of the play recalls these verses from the Bible: 'Judge not, that ye be not judged. For with what judgment ye judge, ye shall be judged: and with what measure ye mete, it shall be measured to you again' (Matthew 7:1–2). The 'Judge not' principle is in the most everyday of Christian prayers, the Lord's Prayer or Our Father: 'Forgive us our trespasses as we forgive those who trespass against us'. Measure for measure is the moral of the New Testament parables about the need to forgive a debtor, as in *The Merchant of Venice*. The mechanisms of *Measure for Measure* are, however, unmeasured: fantastic in the extreme, putting exceptionally hard cases to test issues of justice and mercy. Multiple marriages come as no surprise at the end of a comedy, but there is little romance in those that end *Measure for Measure*. We have not seen mutual love between the marrying couples, with the exception of Juliet and Claudio (recently produced for his sister with his head still on his shoulders). Marriage comes to Lucio as punishment: marriage to a prostitute, awarded by the Duke, whom Lucio has so amusingly traduced throughout the play.

The ending of *Measure for Measure* explicitly recommends equity, 'measure still [always] for measure', and the four final marriages might seem to favour matrimony as a mean between the extremes of the bawdy house and the convent. But how seriously should we take the play? A Duke who has allowed sexual licence to run riot hands his powers to an untried judge who immediately plans judicial rape and murder; these violations of virginity and of life are exchanged for more defensible but equally incredible alternatives by the conjuring tricks of the same Duke, disguised as a friar. Summary brings out the arbitrary nature of the plot, though there is perhaps some similarity with test cases of sexual morality in the Bible: in the story of Susanna and the Elders, Angelo-like judges are executed; the Woman Taken in Adultery of John 8 is told to go and sin no more. The play is satirical about human irresponsibility and folly. Yet its Duke, hovering above the action, seems not to be censured for his criminal irresponsibility; rather, it seems, the merciful exercise of his godlike powers is to be accepted as belonging to his office.

Measure for Measure presents itself at first as a serious play but its plot makes it less so. (The account given here omits several funny scenes set in a louche underworld of bawdy-house rogues, the treatment of which is comic in spirit, though its brothels are sordid and its venereal disease is no joke.) The speed with which the Duke hands down his final arbitrations suggests the impossibility of providing ordinary justice in such extraordinary cases. This is not the wisdom of Solomon but wizardry in ethical, or pseudo-ethical, manipulation of pawns on a human chessboard. As in *The Merchant of Venice*, Shakespeare has taken a simple story and added a deeper human dimension which blazes into life early in the piece, enlisting the sympathies of modern audiences who, accustomed to 'real life' drama, may take plays on such hot issues more literally than did their predecessors. The same problem arises for soft-hearted modern readers of some of Geoffrey Chaucer's tales, for example those of the Clerk and the Franklin. It is said that oral tales need characters with two dimensions, whereas literary fiction needs characters with three dimensions. Plays can be both oral and literary: those of Shakespeare mingle characters in two dimensions with characters in three dimensions, a situation which may cause more difficulty now than it did for audiences who had never read a realistic novel.

Isabella has some fine lines about humanity's unawareness of how its antics look to the eye of heaven, an idea later brandished in King Lear's tirades upon the heath. In pleading for her brother's life, she offers Angelo a general Christian argument upon the perils of office:

> But Man, proud Man,
> Dressed in a little brief authority,
> Most ignorant of what he's most assured,

> His glassy essence, like an angry ape,   [i.e., his soul]
> Plays such fantastic tricks before high heaven
> As make the angels weep ...
>
> (2.2.117–22)

General moral observations of this kind are scattered throughout Shakespeare, especially in *Hamlet*. They raise Shakespeare's plays into universal fables of human nature, and his eloquence can raise our minds to contemplate life's more lasting aspects, however briefly. This side of Shakespeare is real enough, although the best of these 'good sentences' stick in the mind because they arise from the action. The universality of Shakespeare is something to which admirers often testify, though academic criticism has recently completed a 'historicist' phase of trying to relate Shakespeare's texts not to moral wisdom but to historical contexts, usually political.

An awareness of Shakespeare's historical context shows that his contemporaries did often look to literature for moral guidance and ethical wisdom. Although Shakespeare's works are not a magazine of moral counsels, the hope that literature might teach us something about life is still one of the reasons why people read it. *Measure for Measure*, however, is a problem without a solution. It offers examples to avoid rather than to follow, but it does not teach: it blazes, dazzles, baffles, teases.

Measure for Measure is the only 'problem play' which there is space in this book to discuss. *Troilus and Cressida* is a disillusioned treatment of a medieval story, richly retold by Chaucer, of how Cressida, obliged to leave Troy, forsook the love of Troilus for the protection of the Greek Diomede. The play, set in the Trojan War and peopled by Homer's Greek and Trojan heroes, takes a firmly satirical view of Trojan love and Greek heroism. An accomplished, intellectual, anti-romantic play, it has some famous speeches and one scene of painful jealousy. *All's Well That Ends Well* (1605), like *Measure for Measure* and *The Merchant of Venice*, is one of Shakespeare's comedies of love more bitter than sweet: a young woman pursues a man who proves himself consistently unworthy of her; an experimental variation on the romantic norm. After this, Shakespeare ended his increasingly sophisticated and problematic variations on the pre-marital love situation which was the basis of romance comedy; his Sonnets should be included in this set of variations. Although married or mature love features largely in the tragedies to which he now turned, the deeper and darker determination signalled in *Hamlet* is confirmed. All his plays, of whatever genre, now also became more complex, and often larger.

11
Tragedies

Between 1604 and 1608, Shakespeare wrote six tragedies: *Othello* in 1604, in 1605 *Timon of Athens*, in 1605–6 *King Lear*, in 1605–6 *Macbeth*, in 1606–7 *Antony and Cleopatra* and in 1607–8 *Coriolanus*. (*Timon of Athens*, a strange and imperfect play, a play of two halves, was written in collaboration with the young Thomas Middleton. Timon's excessive generosity and patronage bring him to ruin at the end of the first half; in the second, he becomes a self-outcast misanthrope. The play is chiefly notable for its uneven quality and some desolate speeches from Timon, its only memorable character.)

Each of the four greater tragedies, *Hamlet*, *Othello*, *King Lear* and *Macbeth*, ends with the death of the protagonist, but they are not very like each other. One difference is in how far the protagonist is responsible for his situation. *Hamlet* begins with a good man in a bad place from which there is no good way out, a humanist prince in a Gothic prison. In the other plays a pronounced mismatch exists or soon develops between an admired leader and a time which is out of joint. Othello is the victim of intrigue and calumny. In the Britain of *King Lear*, innocence has to go into exile or disguise if it is to survive; yet it was Lear himself who foolishly opened the box of evils. Macbeth's tragedy is almost entirely of his own making: on a hint from the Weird Sisters, and egged on by his wife, a general murders his king and disjoints a whole country. *Coriolanus*, in Shakespeare's last tragedy, is an Achilles, a warrior from the world of epic, in a modern political world of manoeuvre and tactics.

Shakespeare's model of tragedy is not uniform. The four tragedies traditionally regarded as greater have a few elements in common: reduced to an absurd minimum, they are that the protagonist soliloquises, loses his dignity, kills at least one other person, loses at least one relative, and dies. Yet each of the four is properly called tragedy, and the idea of tragedy needs to be looked at before approaching the plays. The notion still persists that the hero of a tragedy has, or ought to have, a 'tragic flaw'. This testifies to the success of the argument of A. C. Bradley's *Shakespearean Tragedy* of 1904. According to Bradley, each of the four tragic heroes has a tragic flaw: ambition in Macbeth, jealousy in Othello; the flaws of Hamlet and Lear take longer to describe. Bradley's book is still worth reading as a one-volume study of this subject, written with consideration, intelligence and knowledge. Its own flaw is that it treats the characters too much as real people, or as people in a realist novel can be treated. Yet a focus on character, though long out of favour with academic critics, is justifiable, since Shakespeare's creation of character by the creation of an idiom for that character is a great part of his hold on later imaginations. Bradley is valued because, like Aristotle, he addressed a major achievement of his native literature and offered a convincing general account of it. The 'tragic flaw' idea works very well for two of the four plays, and the phrase itself has an explanatory power. Simple answers to complex questions are welcome.

Bradley's 'flaw' is related to a key term in Aristotle's analysis, which sought to abstract principles from the practice of the three great Greek tragedians. The Greek word *hamartia*, literally 'missing the mark', here meant 'grave mistake, error of judgement'. Bradley takes this idea, modifies it, and moves it from the field of action to the field of character. Aristotle says little about the character of the protagonist, except that he should be noble yet not so noble that we cannot identify with him (or, as in the case of Antigone, her). Aristotle's analysis is based on the action; he sees the persons of the drama not as characters but as agents. Nor does he see each personage in the drama as having 'a character', a personality, a psychology, as some novelists do. Character for Aristotle is conduct, the sum of a person's acts (a view that is coming back into fashion). He found that tragedy proceeds not from a character flaw, such as jealousy, but from a tragic mistake – as when in Sophocles' *Oedipus the King*, Oedipus, who had been left out to die by his parents at birth, kills a man in a fight after a traffic accident, not knowing that the man is his father, Laius. He then solves the riddle of the Sphinx, and is rewarded by the throne of Thebes, which involves him marrying its queen, Jocasta, not knowing that she is his mother. Although Aristotle's lecture notes do not delve into the detail of single plays, as do Bradley's lectures, an Aristotelian account of *Othello*, for example, might mention Iago and the handkerchief but not speculate about what predisposed Othello to become jealous. Tragedies can be understood without any general theory, but Aristotle's ideas on tragedy inform most later discussions, and Bradley's still affect those of Shakespearian tragedy.

An important difference between Greek tragedy and that of Shakespeare is that in his plays the action is much more the result of human agency than of fate. Shakespeare had a more complex idea of character than is found in Sophocles, Aeschylus or Euripides. As well as human agency, fate and fortune influence the action in Shakespeare, and so does divine Providence. Hamlet says in his last scene, 'there's a divinity which shapes our ends, rough-hew them how we will' (5.2.10–11), and that 'there is a special providence in the fall of a sparrow' (5.2.215–16). So Hamlet sees human agency as affected by a special providence. The editor of an Arden *Hamlet* cites: 'Are not two sparrows sold for a farthing? and one of them shall not fall on the ground without your Father' (Matthew 10:29). He adds: 'The Elizabethans believed both in general providence manifesting itself in the whole system of creation and, within this, in a singular or special providence manifesting itself in the particular event.'[1] More fatalist, less distinctively Christian, is Hamlet's comment, 'the readiness is all' (5.2.218), as he accepts the duel, the arbitration offered by his enemies.

In Sophocles, as already remarked, the *hamartia* of Oedipus is blind: he did not know his parents. Hamlet speaks of shooting an arrow over the house and hurting Laertes. He kills Polonius by mistake, hoping that the spy behind the arras might be Claudius. For Sophocles, the ignorance of Oedipus is no defence: the citizens of Thebes are ritually polluted by its king's unwitting parricide and incest. By contrast, Shakespeare's presentation of tragic action involves post-classical elements: intention, interior disposition, knowledge, free will, conscience. There is Christian guilt as well as shame. Macbeth, for example, understands the gravity of his treason, and thinks of his murder as a sin. He freely chooses to kill Duncan after telling us that Duncan 'is here in double trust', as king and as guest. He even adds that Duncan is not a tyrant who deserves death but a gentle king. Macbeth, in the language of Shakespeare's day, renders himself 'inexcusable'. In an approach to tragedy so based on interior conscience, Shakespeare goes far beyond medieval and earlier Tudor conceptions. *The Mirror for Magistrates* (1559), a bestseller, is, like Chaucer's Monk's Tale, a set of tragedies understood as falls of rulers. Even Sir Philip Sidney took a simple moral 'role model' line, writing that tragedy 'maketh kings fear to be tyrants'. Shakespeare's history plays often show the downfall of tyrants, as in *Richard II* and *Richard III*. His *Julius Caesar* also shows such a fall, followed by the fall of the man who killed Caesar. But *Hamlet* is not a warning against tyranny, and Shakespeare is more than a source of moral examples.

Othello

The tragedies *Romeo and Juliet* and *Julius Caesar* were based on preceding plays or types of play, but Shakespeare's later tragedies are more complex. *Othello* (1604) is closely based on a tale found in an Italian collection of stories. Venice is the setting for the first act, and the rest of the play is set in Cyprus, formerly the eastern outpost of the Venetian empire but now Turkish. Venice here is not a city of merchants but its empire. The honour of those who defend that empire is at stake in what happens. Othello seems to be a *condottiere*, a leader of men, one of the valued professional commanders, often foreign, who served Italian states in their wars. *Condottieri* could change sides, but Othello is markedly loyal to Venice. He says that he is of royal blood – 'I fetch my life and being / From men of royal siege' (1.2.21–2) – confident in himself, in his role, and in his standing in Venice. He says that he need not boast of 'My services which I have done the signiory.' As magnificent in his own way as the magnificoes of Venice, he is a Moor from Morocco and exotically different, therefore, from Desdemona, a white-skinned, blue-veined flower of the Venetian aristocracy. The Moor is more likely to be 'tawny' than a black man from south of the Sahara. The audience probably found it exotic that a Moor whom Desdemona chooses as her lord should also be the governor of Cyprus.[2]

The first scenes of the four great tragedies are arresting, taking us to the heart of the matter, and build to an early climax. The opening scene of *Hamlet* is the most varied and masterly of all openings, but no play begins with so horrible a discord as that which opens *Othello*. Iago, passed over for the post of Othello's 'ensign', or second in command, and moved by jealousy, uses the weak Roderigo to plant a slander where it hurts most. Iago's gross cruelty, in the night scene outside the house of Desdemona's father, Brabantio, is shocking: 'Even now, now, very now,' he yells, 'an old black ram / Is tupping your white ewe' (1.1.89–90). Iago delights in destroying Brabantio's content. Brief as it is, this is as bad as the way he steadily drips slander in Othello's ear through the middle of the play. Iago is also behind the torch-lit arrest of Othello in the next scene; here the victim meets the crisis calmly. The action and setting of the arrest echo at many points the torch-lit arrest of Jesus in the garden of Gethsemane, a scene familiar from all four Gospels. In St Matthew, Jesus commands Peter to put up his sword; Othello says to the men sent to arrest him: 'Keep up your bright swords or the dew will rust them.' This gesture shows a manly nonchalance, the first fine thing in the play, though a quality very different from the humility of the victim in its structural model. A conscious splendour marks Othello's bearing and speech for most of the play. 'She loved me for the dangers I had passed,' he explains to the Duke and the Senate, 'And I loved her that she did pity them.' ('She gave me for my pains a world of sighs', Othello says in the Quarto of 1622; this is usually preferred to the Folio, which reads: 'She gave me for my pains a world of kisses' (1.3.160).) Othello can deal with a direct threat, and knows his value to Venice. But he cannot read Venetian society. His belief that 'Her father loved me' may not be correct. It is remarkable how Shakespeare makes Desdemona's enchantment by this grizzled soldier, a man quite outside her experience, seem entirely explicable. He achieves this by creating for the role a language of peculiar sensuous charm and a melody of cadence that makes its speaker seem exotic. When Iago has played upon Othello long enough, the harmony of his spellbinding language breaks down into incoherent brutality. The glamorous Moor is reduced to 'a beast, that wants discourse of reason' (*Hamlet*, 1.2.152), his armour of honour and respect rendered useless by the filth fed to him by 'honest Iago'.

Iago's management of the plot of *Othello* is malign, but otherwise resembles the way that the actions of *Measure for Measure* and *The Tempest* are managed by dukes who act as the deputies of Providence. Iago's satanic manipulation, both of Othello's imagination and of the business of the handkerchief, renders an unlikely plot quite plausible. A poignant instance of the dramatic irony that arises when the audience knows more than the characters comes when the impulsive Desdemona persists in her plea to Othello to reinstate Cassio as his ensign. Othello had dismissed Cassio after Iago had got the weak-headed ensign drunk in command of the guard. Iago has contrived that Cassio gets the new Governor of Cyprus out of bed on his first night on land with Desdemona since their wedding. Darkness helps Iago in creating the third night-time affray of this night-time play.

Desdemona's pleas (as we know but she does not) confirm her bridegroom in the false belief, fed him by Iago, that she is already having an affair with Cassio, Othello's ensign, a young Florentine, a man closer to her in age, country, race and class. Iago deals in reductive stereotypes. Knowing Desdemona to be innocent, he plays on the loose reputation of the women of Venice. The fate of Desdemona at the hands of Othello, a man normally of decent feeling – 'but yet the pity of it, Iago! O Iago, the pity of it, Iago!' (4.1.193–4) – is one of the most painful things in Shakespeare. Though the setting is exotic, its domestic focus – 'the handkerchief!' – makes *Othello* the closest to home of the tragedies.

The inarticulate, bestial language to which the grandiloquent Othello is reduced is of a kind new in Shakespeare, more deeply degraded than that used by any later character. The cynical, foul-minded non-commissioned officer has pulled the general down to his level; as Othello becomes madder, Iago remains cold and empty. Othello is physically attracted to Desdemona, speaking more than once of her smell. Shakespeare shows elsewhere that he knew of Cyprus as the birthplace of Aphrodite, but the Cyprus of the play is not the place for a honeymoon. In the male world of the garrison we see the likeable Cassio treat the equally likeable courtesan

Bianca as a disposable item. The barely married Desdemona is out of place in a fortress of front-line soldiers. In the camp it becomes credible that the only way in which a proud Moor could deal with a wife whose (supposed) betrayal of him has destroyed his honour – his identity – is to kill her. Late on in the play, Iago's wife Emilia, no angel but a woman who does not think twice before defending Desdemona's integrity, stands forcefully up to male unreason and to her own husband. Female honour is defended with a similarly tonic indignation by Beatrice in *Much Ado*'s Messina and by Paulina in the Sicily of *The Winter's Tale*.

A crux of interpretation remains: how to take Othello's final speech, which affects how we think of him. It is an instance of the tension between character and role, always a problem in drama. Standing by the bed in which he has smothered his wife, Othello is able once more to speak collectedly, recalling in front of representatives of Venice (one of them Desdemona's uncle) the honourable roles he had formerly played as a servant of the state. In this his second speech of self-justification before Venetian authority, he recovers his old command of language, serving to remind them – and us, and himself – of what he once was. He asks them to report what he says to Venice with due care, to set it down. Having recreated the persona which gave him his role, he offers an explanation of how it was that he came mistakenly to kill Desdemona, whom he had loved 'not wisely but too well'; how he was rendered jealous, and 'perplexed in the extreme', and how bitterly he now weeps for his tragic error. This tells his hearers things he needs them to know. But the other motive of Othello's apologia is to distract them so that they should not prevent his suicide. What he speaks becomes, as we increasingly realise, his own funeral eulogy. Othello shows the 'readiness' for death which has been found in tragedy, producing the feelings to which Sidney gave the names 'admiration' and 'commiseration'. This strangely mixed effect is difficult to describe but is perceived in the theatre and by the reader. Othello's final words, though, are meant to be less clear:

> Set you down this;
> And say beside, that in Aleppo once,
> Where a malignant and a turbaned Turk

> Beat a Venetian and traduced the state,
> I took by th' throat the circumcisèd dog
> And smote him – thus.   [*He stabs himself*
>   (5.2.354)

Othello's anecdote of how he once defended a Venetian, and Venice, seems an irrelevant postscript to the report which is to go to Venice; but its recital allows him to draw his weapon to show what he once did in Aleppo, and to achieve his purpose.

All a playwright's words, not only soliloquy and aside, are said for the benefit of the audience. Actors have to say things that are not in character but are demanded by their role in the plot: things which, at a particular juncture, the audience needs to know or to think about.[3] But here Othello speaks very much in character – his old character – to offer a defence of his life. Although such a defence, in one who has served a larger cause, may not be simple vanity, Othello is concerned for the loss not just of 'Othello's occupation' (3.3.350) but of Othello's reputation. He has already claimed that 'nought I did in hate but all in honour', and now says that, though not easily moved to tears, he weeps. Actors have to act, but Othello makes us conscious that he is on a stage, a foreign stage, and on trial. He protests his loyalty to the state in the language of state. The grandeur which Othello creates for his exit both recreates for us the original nobility of his role and darkens our respect for his character.

Iago had, at the beginning of the play, set up Othello's arrest in a scene recalling Gethsemane, Iago playing the part of Judas. Now Othello likens himself to Judas, 'the base Judean', who throws away the pearl richer than all his tribe and afterwards commits suicide.[4] As Othello kills himself, he identifies the enemy of Venice whom he killed in Aleppo as 'a malignant and a turbaned Turk', emphasising Turkish otherness. 'Malignant' might in 1597 recall the notorious treatment of Venice's last governor in Cyprus, Antonio Bragadin, who in 1570 had held Famagusta against a long Turkish siege. Promised honourable treatment if he surrendered, Bragadin was flayed alive. Othello also calls the Turk a 'circumcisèd dog'. Male circumcision was obligatory for Muslims but not for Christians. Though himself a North African, and carrying Africa with him in his voice and appearance, Othello speaks as a champion of Christian Venice. Originally from a part of Africa known as Barbary, from the Berber people of that region, Othello is Christian. Convinced, as the murderer of an innocent wife, that his soul is bound for hell – 'Whip me, ye devils ... Wash me in steep-down gulfs of liquid fire!' – he commits suicide, an act of final despair. In rehearsing his killing of a Turk he may also (so it has seemed to some commentators) seek to destroy the pre-Venetian part of himself, the Egyptian-magic-handkerchief part. Whatever may be said about that, a public speech ending in suicide is supremely a theatrical gesture. Its conclusion – 'And smote him – thus!' [*He stabs himself* ' – makes a terrible silence. All the many analogies evoked in Othello's dying speech fade in the inrush of what follows, to revive again as the tragedy closes.

The story of *Othello* is made intensely dramatic by the characterisation of Othello and Iago. The destructiveness of jealousy is an obvious theme, but a second factor is displacement and its consequences. Othello's occupation is soldiering, and his adopted public identity is Venetian. Placed in a world of personal relations and private manoeuvre unfamiliar to him, Othello's role and identity disintegrate under Iago's torture. (A parallel might be drawn with the tales of displaced identity told by Joseph Conrad, a Polish gentleman, a master mariner in the Merchant Navy, and a novelist in his third language, English.) Othello is an outsider driven mad. Shakespeare part imagined what it would be like to be an outsider with Shylock, but he was limited by the story in which he found Shylock. With Othello, he has an outsider less severely preconceived, less negatively stereotyped, and a story that allows him to imagine the role through to the end.

Hamlet, Prince of Denmark and *King Lear*, raising wider issues, have traditionally been regarded as the greatest of the four major tragedies. *Othello* has a stricter tragic focus than either. *Macbeth* is the shortest, the most headlong of the four. *Antony and Cleopatra*, though truly tragic only in its fifth act, is more lavishly expansive in language and sentiment even than *Hamlet* or *Othello*.

King Lear

King Lear exists in two texts, a Quarto of 1608, which claims to have been the version acted at Court on 26 December 1606, and the Folio text. Later editors combined these texts in the belief that they derived from a common archetype. Some editors now print the two versions separately, as if they were different plays rather than two versions of the same play. The Folio text is shorter by 300 lines. Its cuts and revisions give a less cluttered text for performance without lightening the play's mood.

King Lear is larger than the other tragedies in its moral scope. Indeed it is a play of good and evil, an expanded morality play, a parable with little room for psychological subtlety of characterisation. It begins as a fairy tale. Once upon a time, in ancient Britain, an aged king asked his three daughters to say which loved him best. His youngest, Cordelia, loves him but is not prepared to outbid the protestations of her sisters in order to gain a richer portion of the kingdom. The king prefers flattery to the truth and divides his kingdom in two instead of into three, banishing the daughter who truly loves him – a true tragic error.

The Earl of Gloucester also has good and bad children, though he, like Lear, is misled into thinking that his bastard, Edmund, is true and that his true son Edgar is false. The Gloucester subplot has an equally fairy-tale ending, in which the true Edgar defeats the untrue Edmund in single combat. Virtue triumphs in the minor plot but not in the major. The latter ends with a brief scene introduced by the stage direction *Enter Lear, with Cordelia in his arms*. Lear asks (in the Quarto version):

> Why should a dog, a horse, a rat, have life,
> And thou no breath at all? Thou'lt come no more,
> Never, never, never, never, never.
> Pray you, undo this button. Thank you, sir.
>
> (5.3.308)

Samuel Johnson edited Shakespeare in the 1760s, when he was in his middle fifties. He wrote that he had many years before been so shocked by Cordelia's death that when he came to edit it, 'I know not whether I ever endured to read again the last scenes of the play.' For 'Shakespeare has suffered the virtue of Cordelia to perish in a just cause, contrary to the natural ideas of justice, to the hope of the reader, and what is yet more strange, to the faith of the chronicles.' Johnson's reaction was unusual only in its strength. The Irishman Nahum Tate had in 1681 adapted *King Lear* to restore a happy ending in which Edgar marries Cordelia. This not unskilful version of the play was to hold the stage until 1839. Nahum Tate, whose father was a Puritan clergyman named Faithful, felt no need to be faithful to the text of a secular play; nor did other Restoration writers for the stage. Why does Shakespeare depart from earlier accounts of Lear's reign and, having reunited father and daughter, have Cordelia hanged?[5]

Shakespeare seems in this play to have wished to show the worst pain and the worst evil that could be felt and inflicted by human beings. As usual with him, most of this is conceived in family terms. 'What is the worst?', Edgar asks; and when Lear carries the dead Cordelia onto the stage, Kent asks, 'Is this the promised end?' – a reference to the reversals in the natural order promised for the end of the world at Doomsday. Evil on horseback rides through most of the play. Lear's sufferings when cast out into the storm by his daughters Goneril and Regan drive him mad. Lear's son-in-law Cornwall puts out the eyes of the loyal Duke of Gloucester, sending him 'to smell his way to Dover'. These elder daughters become monsters of cruelty and lust. Edmund, the bastard son of Gloucester, seeks to destroy his brother and his father. The tirades of Lear on the heath, his meeting with Gloucester on the beach, and the play's last scene are terrible to read or to see. The hammer blows of the events take us beyond civilisation to the verge of madness. There is nothing in English like the scenes of Lear, the Fool and Edgar on the heath and on Dover beach. Stretches of *King Lear* reach levels not successfully attempted in other literature in English.

The best does not triumph in *King Lear*, a point so well known that it is sometimes forgotten that the worst does not triumph either. Interpretation of the play is still influenced by productions of the 1960s that assimilated it to the Theatre of Cruelty and Theatre of the Absurd.[6]

Cordelia, Kent and Edgar are good; Goneril, Regan, Edmund and Cornwall are evil. After Cordelia is hanged, Lear dies and Kent is about to follow his master. Edgar is left to say the last lines:

> The weight of this sad time we must obey,
> Speak what we feel, not what we ought to say.

> The oldest hath borne most: we that are young
> Shall never see so much, nor live so long.
>
> (5.3.321–5)

We feel what Edgar says, having seen what suffering humans can bear. Yet evil has lost: Edgar defeats Edmund; Goneril kills Regan and herself. Gloucester, Cordelia, Lear and Kent are dead, the exhausted Edgar and Albany are left standing. We have seen cruelly treated children preserve the lives of their parents: Edgar succours his blinded father, Cordelia her mad father, and both fathers may escape final despair.[7]

In the preface to his *Tess of the d'Urbervilles* (1891), Thomas Hardy presents the words of the blinded Gloucester as Shakespeare's own opinion: 'As flies to wanton boys are we to the gods. They kill us for their sport.' But Gloucester speaks these words in the presence of his wronged son Edgar, who, disguised as a mad beggar, has cared for his father, twice saving him from despair and suicide. Edgar at last discloses himself to his father, whereat, on hearing the true story of his son's conduct, Gloucester's heart 'burst smilingly'. This wincing paradox offers the audience not woe or wonder, but woe and wonder.

Earlier, the maddened and exhausted Lear has been rescued, tended, allowed to sleep, washed, dressed in new garments, and, to the sound of music, brought back to life by his daughter (Act 4, Scene 7). He feels unworthy and foolish and twice asks forgiveness. When they are recaptured by their enemies, and sent to jail together, Lear is delighted:

> Come, let's away to prison:
> We two alone will sing like birds i' th' cage:
> When thou dost ask me blessing, I'll kneel down
> And ask of thee forgiveness ...
>
> (5.3.8–11)

He adds: 'Upon such sacrifices, my Cordelia, / The gods themselves throw incense' (5.3.20–1). Edgar says to the defeated Edmund: 'Let's exchange charity' (5.3.164). Dr Johnson commented: 'Our author by negligence gives his heathens the sentiments and practices of Christianity.'[8] Johnson is struck by this mutual forgiveness but finds it anachronistic in a heathen setting; his historical sense was more developed than Shakespeare's. *Julius Caesar* has a classical ethos – suicide, for example, is no sin – but material details can be wrong. Shakespeare was negligent in having Brutus hear a clock strike three (at 2.1.193). It is reasonable to think that at such a climax Shakespeare was not negligent but knew what he was doing when he introduced contrition and kneeling for forgiveness before showing sacrifice to the gods. Edmund then repents, though too late to save Cordelia. Lear, no longer thinking himself entitled to command, asks a fellow man to undo a button, thanks him and calls him Sir.

The play is a struggle between good and evil – a play, not a moral treatise, but one in which despair is persistently resisted. It has been common since the 1960s, however, to paint the play as entirely despairing: a post-Christian play set in pre-Christian times. But the central story of Christianity does not pretend that we never die, or that goodness is rewarded in this world. Johnson says that the virtue of Cordelia perishes in a just cause. As a Christian, Johnson would have to concede that it can equally be said that Cordelia perishes, but that her virtue does not. That is where Shakespeare leaves the argument, at the point of death, between this world and the next.

It is useful at this point to analyse the penultimate scene of *King Lear* – a glimpse of Shakespeare at work. Before the battle between the army of Cordelia and Lear on the one hand and that of Edmund, Goneril and Regan on the other, Edgar asks his father, Gloucester, to wait for him.

ACT 5, SCENE 2

Alarum within. Enter with drum & colours Lear, Cordelia, & soldiers over the stage; Exeunt.

Enter Edgar disguised as a peasant, guiding the blind Duke of Gloucester.

Edgar:	Here, father, take the shadow of this tree
	For your good host; pray that the right may thrive.
	If ever I return to you again I'll bring you comfort.
Gloucester:	Grace go with you, sir. [*Exit Edgar*

Alarum and retreat within. Enter Edgar

Edgar:	Away, old man. Give me your hand. Away.	5
	King Lear hath lost, he and his daughter ta'en. *taken*	
Gloucester:	No further, sir. A man may rot even here.	
Edgar:	What, in ill thoughts again? Men must endure	
	Their going hence even as their coming hither.	
	Ripeness is all. Come on.	
Gloucester:	And that's true too.	10

[*Exit Edgar guiding Gloucester*

Edgar's farewell in line 3 means that he will do or die. Yet the blind Gloucester's prayers, if any, are not answered; the right does not thrive. Gloucester wishes to stay; like Lear, he does not care whether he is captured. But Edgar will not let his father despair; he reminds him that men must be ready to die, that they cannot choose the moment of their death. The brunt of the scene is given in lines 6 and 10. But the tree adds much: the tree, linked with the words 'rot' and 'ripeness', lends the kindness of lines 1–4 and the counsel of lines 8–10 a faint Christian resonance. The tree helps Edgar remind us that men, like fruit, do not choose to enter the world; and that men should not choose to fall and rot, but be ready for the death God sends. With a tree and some simple words – and with no mention of the trees in Eden or on Calvary – this dramatist can do much in ten lines.

Shakespeare went no deeper in tragedy than *King Lear*. The darkness of *Macbeth*, of *Antony and Cleopatra* and of *Coriolanus* is less universal. Although Macbeth's vivid soliloquies take us so intensely into his mind, his evil is far graver than Lear's selfish arrogance, and the poetic justice refused at the end of *King Lear* is inevitable in *Macbeth*.

Macbeth

Macbeth (1605–6), much the shortest of the tragedies (its text is imperfect, and some mid-to-late scenes are by Thomas Middleton), is addressed to the new king, James, who was now the patron of the King's Men. James VI (of Scotland) had not liked the doctrine of his tutor, George Buchanan, that unjust rulers might justly be deposed. Now also James I of England and of Britain, he had a natural interest in a Scottish play in which a good king is killed in his sleep when a guest of a powerful subject.

There had been attempts on James's life, the last in 1600 in the House of Gowrie. When his mother Mary Queen of Scots was pregnant with him, she had witnessed at close range the end of David Rizzio, her secretary and supposed lover, taken from her own closet at Holyrood House and killed. 'Assassination', an Arabic word, is first found in English in *Macbeth*, but the thing itself was not new. James's father, Darnley, had been blown up and then strangled; he was suspected of the murder of Rizzio. Queen Elizabeth had signed the death warrant for the execution of James's mother. Regicide and succession were never far from the mind of James Stuart when he succeeded to the English throne in March 1603, nor after the Gunpowder Plot of November 1605. James had encouraged English Catholics to expect better treatment than they had had in Elizabeth's later years; but after he had made peace with Spain, he went back on what he had said. James, a survivor of Scottish plots, escaped an English one on 5 November 1605 together with his eldest son; they, with the House of Lords and many judges, were to have been blown up by Guy Fawkes and his associates, disaffected Catholics. The play refers to 'equivocation', a word prominent in the post-Plot trial of a Jesuit in 1606. The play also shows that Banquo's descendants (of whom James was one) would rule for many generations.

Before the murder, Macbeth confesses that his lord and guest is not a tyrant. The sacredness of the king's person is again emphasised by the man who discovers and reports the murder, Macduff:

> Most sacrilegious murder hath broke ope
> The Lord's anointed temple, and stole thence
> The life o' th' building.

$$(4.2.60-3)$$

The image is that of a desecrated temple. Monarchs were anointed at their coronation, like the ancient kings Saul and David, kings of Israel. The king's body is the Lord's anointed temple, and the life stolen from it is sacred. These lines would echo for those in the audience for whom England's temples had been desecrated.[9]

The assassin now asks himself whether the ocean is enough to wash Duncan's blood from his hand, and answers, 'No: this my hand will rather / The multitudinous seas incarnadine / Making the green one red' (2.2.646). The blood on his hand will discolour the ocean: lavish polysyllables shrink to simple monosyllables. Macbeth eventually sinks to the level of the killer he sends to Fife, who says 'What, you egg!' to Macduff's little son before smashing this egg (4.2.80). Towards the end, a man who was once an admired general abuses a servant as a 'cream-faced loon' (5.3.11).

It is a very bloody play. 'Who would have thought the old man to have had so much blood in him?' asks Lady Macbeth (5.1.33–4). Macduff is from his mother's womb 'untimely ripped'. This language is, as the Weird Sisters say, 'thick and slab'. 'Slab' rhymes with 'Bab' and 'Ditch-delivered by a drab' (4.1.30): the finger cut off a baby strangled at birth, an image as horrible as Lady Macbeth's volunteering (at 1.7.57) that she would have dashed out the brains of a baby at her breast rather than break a promise to murder a guest.

Banquo's speech about the blessed microclimate of Macbeth's castle near Inverness shows Shakespeare using dramatic language to do several things at once:

> This guest of summer
> The temple-haunting martlet, does approve
> By his loved mansionry, that the Heaven's breath
> Smells wooingly here. No jutty, frieze,
> Buttress, nor coign of vantage, but this bird
> Hath made his pendent bed and procreant cradle;
> Where they most breed and haunt, I have observed
> The air is delicate.
>
> (1.6.3–10)

There is delicacy in the language of this description of a blessed moment in early summer after the breeding season.[10] We have heard the castle's hostess rejoice that 'The raven himself is hoarse / That croaks the fatal entrance of Duncan / Under my battlements' (1.6.36–8). Editors cite Psalm 84 (Geneva version): 'Yea, the sparowe hath founde her an house, and the swallowe a nest for her, where she maie lay her yong: even by thine altars, o Lord of hostes, my King, and my God.' With the rich compression of his mature work, Shakespeare gives us information, reveals Banquo's character, creates dramatic irony, and contrasts innocence and cruelty. House martins breed; their nestlings shelter in the cradles they build below the battlements under which Duncan enters. Duncan is killed in his sleep for a kingdom which no son of Macbeth will inherit. In the house of the Macbeths there is no breeding, no increase, only killing. Images of birds, small and large, reappear in this play. Tender natural imagery re-enters with the later exchange between Lady Macduff and her son, called her 'egg' by the man who murders them both. Breeding birds again appear after the terrible words 'He has no children', Macduff's reaction to the news that his entire family has been killed by a man sent to his house by Macbeth:

> He has no children. All my pretty ones?
> Did you say all? O hell-kite! All?
> What, all my pretty chickens and their dam
> At one fell swoop?
>
> (4.2.218–21)

Macbeth is a play about murder as a sacrilegious crime against natural and social order. Macduff's reaction stands out from a long and initially puzzling scene, set in England, in which Duncan's son Malcolm repeatedly tests his trustworthiness. Malcolm has had reason to distrust emissaries from Scotland.

Shakespeare is rightly praised for his ability to create character by inventing a speaking voice peculiarly suited to a character. But the generosity of his genius also leads him to do the opposite. A murderer in *Macbeth* is given a speech worthy of Hamlet's friend Horatio. Macbeth has employed three thugs to murder Banquo and, more especially, Banquo's little son Fleance. In this scene, father and son have gone out for a ride before dinner. The killers hide by the roadside in the gloaming to ambush their victims, who are late in returning to the castle:

> *Murderer*: The west yet glimmers with some streaks of day;
> Now spurs the lated traveller apace
> To gain the timely inn.
>
> (3.3.5–7)

Antony and Cleopatra

Antony and Cleopatra is derived, like *Julius Caesar*, from the Life of Mark Antony in Plutarch's *Lives of the Noble Grecians and Romans*. Plutarch's Life begins not long after Antony's victory at Philippi, but in Shakespeare's play Antony's best days are in the past, as is also the case with his Cleopatra, who had borne a son to Julius Caesar. The play is set mostly in the east of the empire, as *Othello* is set in the east of Venice's empire. Antony's reputation, like Othello's, is as a leader of men in war; Cleopatra's reputation is as a successful leader-on of leading men.

The first words of the play, 'Nay, but this dotage of our general's / O'erflows the measure' gives the keynote: a Roman soldier's censure of Antony's 'Egyptian' behaviour, his enslavement to the delights and wiles of Cleopatra. Sexual indulgence or excess was already a theme of the so-called 'Dark Lady' Sonnets, of *Troilus and Cressida* and of *Measure for Measure*. The excesses of immature love formed the theme of the early and middle comedies, in which young lovers recover from their fever, and each is with the right partner when the music stops. This comedy pattern is reversed in *Romeo and Juliet*, and is thereafter resumed less blithely. The lovers are older, and sexual romance has turned into sensual possessiveness, a theme which emerges in *Othello* and dominates *Antony and Cleopatra*. Sexual obsession is something shown in Shakespeare's narrative poems, also featuring classical lovers, as comical, delusive or dangerous. His Sonnets end in some sour epigrams on sexually transmitted disease. He fully suggests the power of sexual possessiveness – but shows that it ends in tears, or that it just ends.

Antony and Cleopatra is not like other plays: its geographical spread and historical backdrop are larger than those of *Hamlet*; only *Cymbeline* is comparably far-flung. The number of persons and places named in the play is very large indeed. Its action moves back and forth across the eastern Mediterranean and Middle East. The background suggests an uncommon knowledge of Roman history and geography, but the question in the foreground is made clear in the first line of the play, even for those who do not know that Octavius is the future Caesar Augustus, the first emperor of Rome. The question is, Can the captivation of Antony by Cleopatra be overcome by the call of Rome and duty? The answer is also clear: Probably not. The theme of the play is often seen as *All for Love; or the World Well Lost*, the title Dryden gave to his rewrite of the play; but it is also about delusion and extravagance, the ordinary world not so well lost. Shakespeare alters Plutarch so that when the play begins Antony's wife Fulvia is still alive. Fulvia's death allows Cleopatra to make an exceptionally catty remark, and allows us to see Antony marry Octavia. This second marriage is a political alliance, but the change shows Antony as a man whose word is not his bond. The tug of war, or tug of love, sways to and fro across the stage for most of the play. Antony has moments of success in battle but foolishly takes Cleopatra's advice to fight at sea, not on the land, where Romans know how to fight. Rome is land based, the sea is unpredictable, Egypt is built on slime, and the 'serpent of Old Nile' has her way. Truths are periodically interjected by the chorus-like figure of Enobarbus, an old soldier, an Iago who really is honest.

The play is not only about love and duty and the destinies of great historical persons. Those who have read *Troilus and Cressida*, or the full sequence of Shakespeare's Sonnets, will know that Shakespeare cannot be cited in support of the idea that amorous infatuation is the route to wisdom – except in comedy. We soon see, if we don't already know, that the uncharismatic Octavius will outmanoeuvre and overcome an opponent for whom politics and war have become part-time occupations. Engaging though Antony can be, most people would rather, if they had to choose, serve in an army or live in a state presided over by the coolly strategic Octavius. Antony and Cleopatra are fascinated by the idea, as well as the physical presence, of each other, and the play is full of magnificent and extravagant compliments to each by the other, though some of the most telling are provided by Enobarbus. (It is worth studying how Shakespeare versified North's English, itself a version of Amyot's French version of Plutarch's Greek.) But Cleopatra and Antony are also fascinated by themselves and by their own images. The games they play fill most of the play with bathos, pathos or comedy – not tragedy. Their words and gestures create glamour; their actions lack grandeur. Honour and reputation are the supreme values of the pre-Christian world, and it is not clear that these sublime egotists preserve them. Their ending is tragic but, compared with those of Hamlet, Othello or Lear, diminished.

Suicide means that they will not be trophies in Augustus Caesar's triumph in Rome. Instead, as death comes near, their thoughts turn to what a social success they will enjoy in the next world: in the Elysian Fields *everyone* will look at them. The celebrity of Antony and Cleopatra, the extravagance with which they indulge their *égoisme à deux*, is their undoing. The flaunting glamour of the play's poetry, gesturing at greatness, has led some readers, in our age of celebrity, to be as captivated as the protagonists themselves are by the mystique of their love. Such readers should read Sonnet 138: 'When my love swears that she is made of truth, / I do believe her though I know she lies' and ends 'Therefore I lie with her and she with me, / And in our faults by lies we flattered be.' Not that the wonderful vitality of the lovers is a delusion: they are loved by their closest followers, and they finally prove that they love one another perhaps more than they love themselves, though Cleopatra dresses up for death. At some point a reader begins to notice how often Antony and Cleopatra allude to their own reputations. The action of *Julius Caesar*, which precedes the action of *Antony and Cleopatra*, ends in Cassius and Brutus successfully getting themselves killed by faithful followers. The protracted failure of Antony to get himself killed in this 'Roman' manner, a sad anticlimax, is also somewhat absurd. It acts, however, like a similar moment in *Romeo and Juliet*, as a foil which enables us to take the later deaths more seriously.

12
Late Romances

The sequence of composition of the plays leading up to *The Tempest*, known as the late romances, is as follows:

1607–8	*Pericles*
[1607–8	*Coriolanus*]
1609–11	*The Winter's Tale*
1610–11	*Cymbeline*
1611	*The Tempest*

These plays mark a decided change of tack from the series of tragedies which ends with *Coriolanus*. The first of them, *Pericles*, written in collaboration with George Wilkins, survives only in a poor and pirated copy. Omitted from the First Folio, it was dismissed by Ben Jonson as 'a mouldy tale'. It would not appeal to Jonson's classical taste, for it is a popular story of an old-fashioned kind, a romance derived from *Apollonius of Tyre*, of the third century, late in the Hellenistic period of Greek literature, one often recycled in the Middle Ages. Shakespeare relies on a version by Chaucer's contemporary, John Gower, and the play has a Prologue spoken by Gower in a medieval kind of English verse, a signal to the audience to expect an old-fashioned romance. He changes the name of the King of Tyre from Apollonius to Pericles, a name he found in a modern 'Greek' pastoral romance, Sidney's *Arcadia* (the source also of the Gloucester subplot to *King Lear*). Shakespeare had already drawn on *Apollonius of Tyre* for *The Comedy of Errors* and *Twelfth Night*. *Pericles* is an odd play, with some moving final scenes. It is full of unwelcome partings and welcome reunions – sea journeys, shipwrecks, the loss of wife and child and a reunion a generation later. This formula more or less covers the other three late romances: all four turn on the relation of father and lost children, especially of father and daughter. The tales of Chaucer's Franklin, Clerk and Man of Law are miraculous romances of a similar kind. Shakespeare's romances or tragicomedies differ so much from the plays that precede them and are so like each other that they form a distinct set.

The first person to identify these plays as romances was Edward Dowden in 1877, a perception made possible after scholars had agreed a chronology of Shakespeare's output. The change from tragic endings to comic endings is unmissable, and the happy endings of these romances are of a fairy-tale kind. Commonsense moralists like Dr Johnson, who believe that art should plausibly reflect real life as it ordinarily happens, have thought that Shakespeare was losing his grip, as do sceptics such as Lytton Strachey. The success of novels of detailed realism have made such lengthy narratives seem more true to ordinary life than a three-hour play – yet the reality pretended by literature of any kind is a pretence, a pretence which the consumers of literature keep up. This is one application of Touchstone's saying that 'the truest poetry is the most feigning' (*As You Like It*, 3.2.15). A detailed simulacrum of humdrum ordinary life is just as artificial as a fairy tale, though the dominance of realist fiction has accustomed us to take realist fiction more seriously than fairy fiction. Critics less wedded to normative realism and more open to mysterious exceptions to natural order, to imaginative possibility, to the role of symbolic or metaphysical analogy, have placed a high value on the late romances. This happened in the mid-twentieth century in the writings of Wilson Knight, of T. S. Eliot and of W. H. Auden. Of these four plays only *The Winter's Tale* and *The Tempest* are very often performed. *Cymbeline*, the most miscellaneous and extravagantly experimental of the four, receives much critical attention.

Shakespeare's plays never state a view, but the romances mark a new orientation of interest. Shakespeare may have had no more tragedies to write, but his turn back to romance may have been affected by two practical factors, one theatrical, the other biographical. First, from 1609, the King's Men began to perform in the indoor Blackfriars theatre as well as at the outdoor Globe. Indoor performance, which gave them a reliable winter season, required candlelight, and intervals in which the candles were renewed. Candlelight is conducive to a dreamier performance style than daylight. Music played a greater part, and we know that woodwind rather than brass was used at Blackfriars. A less broad style of acting also seems likely. The audience paid more, and was more select. Gods and goddesses begin to appear in these romances, as do dances, both features of the masque – an elaborate and expensive kind of show, new and popular at court. Secondly, Shakespeare's family changed personnel as he began to write these plays. In 1607 his youngest brother, Edmund, died at the age of 27. Edmund was an actor in London, as William had been for 27 years or more. His father had died in 1601, and in 1608 his mother Mary died. William must have expected that he would be the next Shakespeare to go. It was 12 years since the death of his son Hamnet, but he had two daughters in their twenties. Indeed, 1607 was the year in which his first child, Susanna, married a Stratford physician – and produced a daughter, Elizabeth, the only grandchild he would see. Regeneration is the subject of the late romances. A young writer often writes about love in the young, so it is not a surprise if a writer whose daughter marries should write about fathers and daughters – not that one can simply read across from work to life and vice versa, not with this shadowy writer.

The strong and often subversive role played by sexual attraction in Shakespeare's writing from *Hamlet* onwards reaches a kind of terminus in *Antony and Cleopatra*. The Sonnets, *Hamlet, Troilus and Cressida, Measure for Measure, Othello* and *King Lear* show the power of sexual passion to destroy other ties. Hamlet's attacks on the power of women over men is a sign of unbalance. In his madness, Lear reasons that since his children have persecuted him there should be no more children, no more procreation. When Macbeth hesitates to kill Duncan, his wife taunts him with lack of manliness. Iago tests Othello's masculine honour with tales of Desdemona's adultery. Antony weighs honour and sexual love in a more tragicomic balance. Children would be out of place in *Julius Caesar* or *Antony and Cleopatra*, and the relation of children to a tragic protagonist is crucial only in *King Lear* and (negatively) in *Macbeth*. It now became central. Shakespeare's last tragedy, *Coriolanus*, turns on the relationship of the adult Coriolanus to his mother, Volumnia.

Late in *King Lear*, the moves of Edmund, Goneril and Regan are driven by eagerness to possess, to take, whereas Cordelia's care for her father is nothing but giving. She revives him, brings him, as he says, back out of the grave – and is then hanged. The moral resurrection of a father by means of a daughter better than he deserves is a theme in four of the last five plays Shakespeare wrote before he spent more time in Stratford: *Pericles*, *Cymbeline*, *The Winter's Tale* and *The Tempest*. They offer what can be seen as alternative endings to *King Lear*, where this theme is first announced, in response, as it were, to the cruelty of Cordelia's hanging. Tragedy is rewritten as comedy, as *Lear* was to be by Nahum Tate. Earlier, *Romeo and Juliet*, ending in a tragic double suicide, was followed by *A Midsummer Night's Dream*, ending in a double suicide treated as farce. Sexual jealousy as a major theme is confined to the first half of *The Winter's Tale*, where it is reduced to its irrational extreme, since Leontes' jealous suspicion of his wife's fidelity is (unlike the jealousy of earlier plays) entirely self-generated. He asks her to win his friend over to stay longer; then misconstrues her actions as the stuff of his nightmares.

The Winter's Tale

The Winter's Tale is a play framed in contrasting halves of domestic tragedy and pastoral comedy. The first is set in Sicily in winter; the second, introduced by Time as chorus, 16 years later, opens towards harvest time on 'the sea coast of Bohemia'. Shakespeare draws attention to the symmetry of this improbable yarn, a tale for the winter fireside, by placing a theatrical exclamation mark towards the end of Act 3, in a famous stage direction: *Exit, pursued by a bear*. The man making this very final exit is Antigonus, whose ship has gone down in a tempest with the loss of all hands. The eating of the virtuous, noble Antigonus takes place offstage, as is observed by a young shepherd, who tells his father: 'the men are not yet cold under water, nor the bear half dined on the gentleman: he's at it now' (3.3.103–5). Arbitrariness is a regular if unpredictable aspect of the world's arrangements, but these tragic facts are rendered with a comic grotesqueness – 'he's at it now' – that reminds us that we are at a play.

As the play opens, Leontes, King of Sicilia, asks his wife Hermione to do all she can to persuade his childhood friend, Polixenes of Bohemia, to prolong his stay with them. Leontes then misinterprets one of their exchanges and wildly accuses her of open infidelity, in words that recall Hamlet's charges against his mother. When Hermione, with superb dignity, denies this, he declares that 'Your actions are my dreams' (3.2.82). His jealous fit causes his son and heir Mamillius to die of shock at hearing of the accusation. The boy's name means male child at the breast. News of her son's death appears to kill Hermione also; she faints when she hears it. Leontes seems to have destroyed his whole family, for, thinking the girl-child to which Hermione has just given birth is her bastard by Polixenes, Leontes says first that the bastard should be burnt, but then orders Antigonus to get rid of it, to expose it to die.

Leontes is withstood by Paulina, Hermione's lady-in-waiting, in much the same way as Cordelia, Kent and the Fool withstand the tyranny of King Lear. Paulina does so with the force of Beatrice or Emilia and more grandly; but, as it seems, to little avail. Although he is convinced that he is justified, Leontes sends to ask the oracle at Delphos (Delos) to confirm this. But the oracle responds: 'Hermione is chaste; Leontes a jealous tyrant; his innocent babe truly begotten; and the king shall live without an heir, if that which is lost be not found' (3.2.131–6). The oracle is remarkably unambiguous, until its final clause. This 'if' clause supports Hermione in her shamming of death, and illuminates the lost daughter's name, which we are later told is Perdita (Latin for 'lost girl'). Leontes does 16 years of penance, during which Paulina pretends that Hermione is indeed dead. This is like the sham death of Hero in *Much Ado*, and not unlike the Duke's juggling in *Measure for Measure*. In Shakespeare's comic romances, certain men and women are allowed to play God, often God as Joker. This stage Providence is someone of authority, whether official or moral: a Duke, disguised or deposed; or a woman defending a falsely accused woman.

In Act 2, Scene 1, Hermione says to Mamillius:

>   Pray you, sit by us,
> And tell 's a tale.
> *Mamillius*:   Merry or sad shall 't be?
> *Hermione*:   As merry as you will.
> *Mamillius*:   A sad tale's best for winter ...
>   (2.1.25)

This innocence in a rapidly darkening world recalls Lady Macduff and her son. The play's career into nightmare ends in the bear's jaws – but this is followed by the shepherds' discovery of a 'thing new-born' (3.3.113), the baby girl dropped by Antigonus. The lost girl, Perdita, is brought up a shepherdess; she eventually becomes the beloved of Florizel, son of king Polixenes. A long and flowery pastoral idyll, in which the young lovers become engaged, is interrupted by a disguised Polixenes. An unrecognised king debates with a girl who does not know that she is a princess as to whether nobility comes from birth or from upbringing. Polixenes then argues with Florizel, who declares that he intends to marry this shepherdess without his father's permission. Angered, the king throws off his disguise, but the play is now on its comic upswing and all ends well: the loyal counsellor Camillo sends the young lovers to Sicily, to Leontes, where there is a magical ending in the famous and improbably beautiful statue scene, in which Leontes has both his wife and daughter restored to him. The bastard to be burnt turns out to be a princess to be bred from. Nature, a female deity, is good.

This play is one in which 'all losses are restored and sorrows end' (Sonnet 30). All ends very well indeed. What's done can be undone, with all the poetic justice Dr Johnson felt cheated of in *King Lear*. Not all is rosy: Mamillius is dead, Antigonus has been eaten, and Leontes has had 16 years of purgatory on earth, though this is largely forgotten in the miraculous restoration of wife and daughter. (We are not asked to think about Hermione's 16 years in limbo.) Shakespeare makes these deeply desired outcomes more acceptable by adding to his source a character who stands outside the action and comments disbelievingly upon it. In earlier plays this was the role of comic servants, then of Falstaff (one side of him), of the melancholy Jaques, of the Fools. The effect is to immunise the audience against disbelief by voicing it within the play. Here the mocker is the rogue Autolycus, a character taken from Ovid. His name can mean 'the wolf itself', and Autolycus preys upon the innocents of the pastoral world.

The late romances have a religious dimension which shows more than in most other Shakespeare plays, partly because these romances draw attention to what they share with myth, fable and parable. The names of three of the daughters are pointedly symbolic: Perdita (lost girl), Imogen/Innogen (innocence), Marina (girl from the sea). The fourth daughter, Miranda, has a name which, as the text of *The Tempest* points out three times, means 'she who is to be wondered at'.[1] The names are generally allegorical rather than Christian, and the deities who appear in these plays are pagan. The direct representation of Christian subjects, the subject matter of drama until Shakespeare's youth, was forbidden by law on the Elizabethan and Jacobean stage. Pagan mythology, however, after the Roman Empire accepted Christianity in the fourth century, was gradually assimilated and given Christian senses. Sophisticated writers could in certain contexts use 'Jove' as a name for God. This practice, known as Christian syncretism, became a norm in European literature, art and music. It was employed by Chaucer and by Protestant writers such as Spenser, and by many writers known to Shakespeare; also by the young Milton and by Dryden and later writers too. Syncretism used pagan myth allegorically, in much the same way as episodes in the Old Testament were seen as foreshadowing Christian revelation. Shakespeare never writes quite in this way, even in the late romances, but his classical deities are not simply pagan; their context dips them in a mild solution of Christian humanism, and the dye is visible.

Any effort to read Shakespeare historically has to come to terms with the role of religion in the culture of his day as a given – a latent presence, a potentiality. Readers today for whom religion is not a given may not see the Christianity which can colour his words. Although religious subject matter was banned by law from popular stages, and Elizabethan drama is therefore human and secular, religious ways of thinking could not be banned. The language available to Shakespeare is shot through with 30 to 40 generations of Christian literacy. Such a generalisation may be accepted as valid history, yet readers who bring little knowledge of Christianity to Shakespeare may miss its quieter traces, and discount explicit terms as merely conventional. To take an example, in the final speech of *Macbeth*, the victorious Malcolm refers to the Macbeths as 'this dead butcher and his fiend-like queen'. Harsh terms in a victor's mouth are to be expected. Yet 'fiend-like' is not conventional: Lady Macbeth calls on 'murderous ministers' to 'unsex' her, commanding demons to replace the milk in her 'woman's breasts' with bitter gall.

'Angels and ministers of grace defend us!' exclaims Hamlet (1.4.39). In the late romances the daughters are ministers of grace, and the word 'grace' recurs in various senses. The unangelic Angelo had said to the Duke in *Measure for Measure*, 'When I perceive your grace, like power divine, / Hath looked upon my passes ...' (5.1.366–7). Here 'grace' is the form of address for a duke; 'like power divine', however, recalls 'grace' as a Christian term for divine help, a key term in Reformation controversies. Although Western Christendom had begun to break up before Shakespeare's birth, he and his audience lived in a world in which Christian assumptions shaped understanding. He was born in an old-fashioned milieu and brought up in a culture habituated to symbol and analogy rather than to literalism, though his plays rarely invoke theology.[2] The miracles in these plays – the survival of exposed infants, the statue scene – are stage miracles: transformation scenes accompanied by music, whose origins are in secular fairy tale, not Christian legend. The agents are coincidence and every form of improbability. The lost are found, wrongs can be righted, death is not separation, families are reunited in love. The happy endings are providential: they come as a grace but embodied in human forgiveness and loving-kindness. The plane of action is natural, human and familial, but with explicitly supernatural interventions, pagan in name yet not without some Christian meaning. There is much specifically Christian kneeling, repentance and forgiveness, and grace is often mentioned. Religious gestures and terms are part of the effect.

As a dramatist Shakespeare deals in human experience – here in family conflict, love and reconciliation between generations – and his miracles are human miracles in narratives arranged by himself. Robustly virtuous characters such as Kent, Edgar, Antigonus, Paulina and Camillo are agents in the action; and yet the restorative effect of the recovered daughters, and of Hermione, comes as a providential kind of grace, not as a reward for merit on the part of a father. In the light of the tradition of Christian syncretism outlined above, the intermittent but persistent religious quality of these plays can be seen as less moral than symbolic and providential. Generational conflict is magicked into regeneration and peaceable succession. But the mysterious agencies involved are explicitly supernatural, and the use of Christian language, gesture and analogy is not supplementary to the plane of human action but part of it. Commentators on Shakespeare cite the impact of Niccolò Machiavelli on Tudor political thinking, and note that relativist ideas voiced by Shakespeare characters are also found in Michel de Montaigne. Yet such materialism and scepticism are not quite like those of today.

It is necessary to state firmly that Shakespeare's was not an age in whose general culture the secular and religious had become systems of understanding of human life so distinct and separate as to be opposed or thought incompatible. Exceptions test rules, and Edmund's initial soliloquy in *King Lear*, 'Nature, be thou my goddess', is an exception which confirms this generalisation as generally true. It is certainly also the case that the endings of these late plays look to the future with a hope quite absent from the exhausted end of *Lear*.

The Tempest

The three predecessors of *The Tempest* begin with tragedy and end in comedy: the father is eventually restored to and by the daughter. But in this play the tragic matter is already in 'the dark backward and abysm of time' (1.1.50). Twelve years have passed since Prospero, Duke of Milan, excessively devoted to his magical studies, was overthrown, and put into a leaky boat with his three-year-old daughter and his book. He sees her as an angel: 'A cherubin / Thou wast, that didst preserve me' (1.1.152–3). Divine Providence brings them to a desert island, where the action of the play embodies and resolves a central issue in (Christian) humanism: how far can education and upbringing cure the imperfections of human nature?

The play is an original myth, in which Prospero educates his daughter but fails to educate a strangely shaped creature met on the island, Caliban, whom he calls 'a devil … in whose nature nurture will never stick' (4.1.188–9). Caliban had tried to rape Prospero's daughter, hence Prospero's anger. Prospero uses magic to raise the tempest and bring onto the island a passing ship which, he has divined, carries back from Tunis the very men who overthrew him – his brother Antonio and Alonso, King of Naples – along with Alonso's brother Sebastian and son Ferdinand. He uses the airy spirit Ariel, also found on the island, to test these courtly castaways. Ferdinand proves worthy of Miranda's hand; Alonso repents his crime; but Antonio and Sebastian, younger brothers, have no wish to reform. They are like Edmund Spenser's Gryll, a man transformed by enchantment into a pig, who, when offered the chance to return to human shape, prefers to remain a pig. Book II of *The Faerie Queene* concludes 'Let Gryll be Gryll, and have his hoggish mind'. Antonio and Sebastian, who plot to murder the sleeping Alonso, joke about how much money they might make out of marketing Caliban as a fish. At the end of the play Caliban (who has plotted to murder Prospero) resolves (unlike the hoggish nobles) to 'be wise hereafter, / And seek for grace' (5.1.298–9). Prospero resigns his magic, and will return to Naples to see the wedding of Ferdinand and Miranda, 'And thence retire me to my Milan, where / Every third thought shall be my grave' (5.1.314).

The Tempest stands first in the Folio, with more stage directions than other plays. Perhaps it was a notable success; it certainly seems to have been the last play Shakespeare wrote solo, written with particular care, in a mode of its own. *The Tempest* has inevitably been taken as a testament, and Prospero as the author bowing out. Shakespeare seems thereafter to have spent more time in his large house in Stratford, and cut his work to part-time collaboration with John Fletcher on three further plays. During a performance of *Henry VIII* the discharge of a cannon set fire to the thatch of the Globe, which burned down and was then rebuilt.

Prospero takes the duke-in-charge figure to new heights. The Duke in *Measure for Measure* played Providence in disguise, but Prospero is a 'white' magician who openly creates and directs the action. He is in this like his creator, the player-poet-playwright-impresario who had likened the world to a stage. After the masque of Hymen (with Iris, Ceres and Juno) which Prospero puts on for the benefit of Ferdinand and Miranda, Prospero says:

> Our revels now are ended. These our actors,
> As I foretold you, were all spirits, and
> Are melted into air, into thin air;
> And like the baseless fabric of this vision,
> The cloud-capped towers, the gorgeous palaces,
> The solemn temples, the great globe itself,
> Yea, all which it inherit, shall dissolve;
> And, like this insubstantial pageant faded,
> Leave not a rack behind. We are such stuff
> As dreams are made on, and our little life
> Is rounded with a sleep.
>
> (4.1.148–58)

'The great globe itself' is the theatre as well as the world it represented. Prospero ceremoniously abjures his 'rough magic' and drowns his book. Gonzalo invokes a blessing on the young couple, using a theatrical metaphor: 'Look down, you gods, / And on this couple drop a blessed crown, / For it is you that have chalked forth the way / Which brought us hither' (5.1.203–6). Directors still use chalk to 'block' on the boards of the stage the moves the actors are to make. If the world is a stage, the author is a god who makes the providence of the plot.

The Tempest, like *A Midsummer Night's Dream*, is a play which relies upon the image-making powers of language, and the transforming power of musical sound. The earthy speech in which Caliban describes the island, though it has written sources, is original in its expression. Shakespeare's ear, and linguistic invention, create distinctive idioms for Caliban and Ariel. These symbolic creatures posed a challenge more difficult in some ways than creating the idiom of, say, Shylock or Othello, for whom he may have had partial models in people he had heard speak; or of Puck, a figure from English folklore. Ariel, Caliban's airy counterpart, is, like Puck, a spirit who sings and works the transformations commanded by his master. At the end of the play he is released, and in the final words of the Epilogue Prospero too asks the audience ask to 'set me free'.

The action of *The Tempest* begins its father–daughter story at a much later stage than do *King Lear* or the other late romances. Lear, cured of his madness, liked the idea of prison with Cordelia: 'we two will sing alone like birds in the cage'. *The Tempest* opens, after the storm in its title, with an old father and young daughter singing alone in the cage of the island, though it is the father who does most of the talking. His tale of past traumas is an involved one, but he clearly has magical powers. The tragic part of the story, which took up half of the play in *Pericles*, *The Winter's Tale* and *Cymbeline*, is over. The backstory is told by Duke to daughter in an expository Act 1, Scene 2, a static contrast to the opening action of the storm which Ariel created on Prospero's orders. Although the mind of the magus is as distempered as the elements he disturbs, his tempest and his exposition show him as master of the island. No new plot to do away with him will succeed.

This ceremonious romance, full of magical song and poetry, dance and symbolic gesture, with spirits of the air and of the earth, ends with the appearance of a masque, with goddesses, to bless the engagement of Miranda and Ferdinand. (Masques at King James's court ended with nobles in the audience coming to take part in the final dance, though they did not speak. *The Tempest*, we know, was played at Court in 1611.) Its mode is at the opposite pole to realism, even in the farcical episode of the drunken servants and the moon-calf: it is a fairy tale, a magic fable, a secular parable; transparent in places, mysterious in others. Prospero's expository lecture functions as a prologue placed not before but after the opening scene; yet the play itself observes the Unities. Act 1, Scene 2 is so like a lecture that every 20 lines Prospero asks Miranda (the audience) whether she is listening: a comic version of the questions put by Socrates in the dialogues of Plato. The final effect of *The Tempest* is like that of a baroque saint's legend or secular nativity play, in which the 'sacred' central revelation is the ideal love of Miranda and Ferdinand '*discovered … playing at chess*', a romance rewrite of a humanist, unfallen Garden.

Compared with its 35 extant predecessors, this play, *The Tempest*, is simple, its plot hardly more than a diagram, though its fable is not without mystery or depth. Like *King Lear*, it is a play of mere good and evil, innocence and experience, candour and cunning, and also a family story: the care of father for daughter, and the love of Miranda and Ferdinand. This very young love, carefully overseen by Prospero, is made innocent, almost colourless, without the heat of Romeo and Juliet. In contrast with earlier comedies, bawdy humour is almost entirely absent, though Caliban says of his foiled rape, 'Oh ho, Oh ho! Would't had been done!' (1.2.351). Ideal innocence and parental safeguards are, as in Milan in the past, menaced by treason, mutiny and murder, plotted first by two nobles, then by two drunken servants and a drunken Caliban.

Prospero's purposes in exercising his authority are corrective and educative, despite the tempest that beats in his mind, despite his testiness and the distance at which he keeps Ferdinand. The point of his tempest is, by making Alonso think his son is drowned, to get the king to repent; also to make sure the king's son is suitable for Miranda. Prospero is fierce with Caliban, a mysterious and unclassifiable creature, not native to the island but brought there by the witch Sycorax, his 'dam' (not 'mother'), before the arrival of Prospero and Miranda. Caliban's father is said to be a devil. Caliban is called a fish, a cat, a tortoise, a mooncalf, a fishy monster, a demi-devil, and, once, a man. Today he is usually played for pathos and/or nobility; in 1611 he would have come on as a kind of comical pantomime monster. He is more animal than human, unable to speak until Prospero teaches him the human privilege of speech, an ability identified with the reason which defines humanity. He embodies the animal side of human nature, being given lovely speeches about things of nature, the physical resources of the island, which he had showed to Prospero. He hears music, a good sign, saying to the drunken Stephano, 'Be not afeard. The isle is full of noises, / Sounds and sweet airs, that give delight and hurt not' (3.2.138–9).

With the end of European empires in the mid-twentieth century came an historical perspective in which *The Tempest* might be applied to colonisation, and Prospero seem not imperious but imperialist.[3] Previous to this time, Prospero's magic had been seen as 'white' and good, in contrast to Sycorax and her black magic. Prospero could now be seen as white and bad. Politics, however, are explicit in the play only when the idea of a commonwealth without a sovereign is floated by Gonzalo, to take the minds of his superiors off their plight; but Alonso is too grief-stricken to listen, and the others too cynical.

The island is all Miranda knows. When she sees her first men, other than her father and Ferdinand (and Caliban, if Caliban is a man), she famously exclaims, 'O brave new world / That has such people in it' (5.1.186–7). The 'new world' Miranda wonders at is not the transatlantic New World but a world which has men in it. Her father's memorable response, ''Tis new to thee', is made in the knowledge that these 'brave' men include the 'men of sin' who had sent Miranda to drown. Shakespeare's invented plot draws on analogues from Virgil, Erasmus, Ariosto, the *commedia dell'arte* and travel literature. It alludes also to stories of a recent voyage in which an English ship was driven onto Bermuda, described as a quasi-paradisal island, whose helpful inhabitants allowed the English to repair their boats and go on to Virginia. Europeans had since 1492 debated whether the New World was innocent, or populated by violent savages, or was something between the two.

The island in the play, however, lies between Tunis and Naples, not between Plymouth and Jamestown, and Sir Frank Kermode, who had edited the play, reaffirmed, late in his long career, that 'Caliban is really the *homo selvaticus* of European tradition, with additional New World details' (*selvaticus* = 'savage'; originally 'of the woods').[4] Humanists debated whether a creature such as Caliban, not brought up by humans, might learn to master 'discourse of reason', language. Columbus's 'discovery' of the Bahamas rekindled debate at a moment when European humanists were working on the idea that a liberal education could radically improve human nature, and reason it out of its originally fallen condition. On the fictional island of Thomas More's *Utopia* (No-Placia), men and women are rational and unfallen, as they once were in the Garden of Eden.

Prospero's island is fictional and theatrical, not historical, but, as with *The Merchant of Venice*, it is historical retrospect that makes us flinch when Prospero calls Caliban 'savage' and 'slave'. The success of *The Tempest* has made its story so familiar that it is now a myth, recast for other media such as film or opera. The myth of *The Tempest* is like the story of *Robinson Crusoe*: a white man cast on an island meets an existing inhabitant. *The Tempest* was one of the Shakespeare plays most often adapted for new theatres after 1660. As myth or story, it lends itself to political allegorising: parts of it recall some of the sadder scenes of global colonial history.

Caliban tries to rape his master's daughter; the sailors' grog makes him drunk; his rebellion fails; he uses his newly learned language in order to curse, though also for better ends.

But readers of Shakespeare's *Tempest* do not read a myth but a text. The play assumes a hierarchical world: Caliban, the off-spring of a devil and a witch, is at the bottom; next is Ariel, a spirit of the air. Above, are four goddesses. Between, mankind: masters, sailors, servants. Species and ranks are not equal: the ladder of creation goes from irrational lower animals up to the angels via rational humans. Caliban, though not native to the island, was at one time its sole free inhabitant, since Ariel had been pinned in a tree by Sycorax before her death. Prospero used magic power to free Ariel and later, after the attempted rape of his child, to enslave Caliban. What we are told of Caliban's parentage makes him sub-human, though the ending, as we shall see, points upwards.

The Tempest is a tale of wonder, not an Orwellian political fable. In the period 1601 to 1611, Britain had an overseas colony in Ireland and a toehold at Jamestown, Virginia. Its ships cruised for the colonial gold of other Christians in the Caribbean. But the play's island, if anywhere, is between Naples and Tunis, like the islands of the enchanting Calypso and the enchantress Circe on which Odysseus landed. Like Homer's islands, this is a fantasy island: not Bermuda, not a plantation, not on a map. It is, like More's Utopia, an island of the mind. It is not, however, 'utopian' in the modern sense, for no amount of moral education would lead the Gryll-like Antonio to reform. The sophisticated mockery and amusing cynicism of the two unpersuaded nobles are there to counteract the wish fulfilment of the plot, and make it accept-able. In a manoeuvre of a kind previously noted, Shakespeare puts in such Lucio-like doubters to voice our own incredulity, and to relieve it. This is a play made for our delight, not to raise our political consciousness; the issues it proposes – indirectly – are moral and cultural. Politics, so far as they enter into the play, are seen from the higher ground of a moral philosophy focused on the moral educability of human beings. Finally, unlike the two cynical noblemen, Caliban, as we have seen, says, 'I'll be wise hereafter, / And seek for grace' (5.1.294).

Prospero's anger against those who sought to kill him and his daughter has now been allayed, and he had been led to this change of heart by his better spirit, Ariel, who bases his argument on reason, the guiding principle of classical Christian humanism:

Ariel: … Your charm so strongly works 'em
            That if you now beheld them your affections
            Would become tender.
Prospero: Dost thou think so, spirit?
Ariel: Mine would sir, were I human.
Prospero: And mine shall …
            … with my nobler reason 'gainst my fury
            Do I take part …

(5.1.15–25)

After *The Tempest*, Shakespeare collaborated with John Fletcher upon three plays: *Henry VIII*, also known as *All is True*; *The Two Noble Kinsmen*; and the lost play *Cardenio*, which dramatised a romantic/sensational episode from Cervantes' *Don Quixote*. The other two plays are well worth reading and seeing. *Henry VIII* deals eloquently with the downfall of Wolsey and Katherine, richly reworking the fall theme of his earliest history plays. *The Two Noble Kinsmen* is a sentimental and comic reworking of Chaucer's Knight's Tale, on which Shakespeare had already drawn in *A Midsummer Night's Dream*. Shakespeare did the grand side, Fletcher the comic-sentimental side.

13
Retrospect

William Shakespeare had extraordinary gifts, and the luck to arrive in the theatre at an extraordinary moment. What he made, what he achieved, still seems wonderful. Like Mozart, he found composition easy, which is not to say that he did not push himself. He preferred to complicate existing plays and stories, inventing and transforming as necessary. He perfected the new genre of the history play, and developed new forms of romance and sexual comedy. After *Henry VI*, each play is different; this is especially true in tragedy and in the later work. To read through Shakespeare's plays is to meet an unprecedented range and variety of situations, behaviour and sentiment, and to improve understanding of possible human actions and reactions, as experienced and seen from a succession of points of view. This understanding of multiple human interaction, seen from all sides, is a new thing in English literature, anticipated in Chaucer but rarely reapproached in later writers. An enriching sense that we can understand and feel what each character in a situation thinks and feels is perhaps Shakespeare's most remarkable gift to us. If human lives have materially changed, human nature has changed less. This introduction to half of Shakespeare's plays has sometimes had to point to places in which the blend of conditions and assumptions of our time do not coincide with those of his. As Johnson wrote in his Preface, 'Every man's performances, to be rightly estimated, must be compared with the state of the age in which he lived.'[1] The relation to historical conditions has to be considered, elusive as it often is. But historicism has its limits: it is a fact that Shakespeare's works have for four centuries been found valuable by a wide variety of people, not only by his compatriots or by English speakers. To vary Ben Jonson's words, Shakespeare was of an age but is also for all time. At the outset of this book, Samuel Johnson's verdict was quoted: that by reading Shakespeare 'a hermit could estimate the transactions of the world'. Since Johnson's day the novel has added detail and breadth to our idea of the world's transactions. But the novel also adds length, and Johnson's hermit would miss the concentrated force of drama, the melody of Shakespeare's verse and the richness of his thought and language.

Shakespeare's supposed point of view

John Keats was to praise Shakespeare's 'negative capability', his non-partisan and un-ideological capacity; something which Leo Tolstoy and G. B. Shaw saw and disliked. Shakespeare has been claimed as a supporter of the most diverse points of view, political and social, and the lines he wrote for actors to speak are taken as evidence of his own attitudes. If this were reliable evidence, Shakespeare had a very wide range of attitudes. But speeches written for actors are not evidence of an author's attitudes, but rather of his capacity. It is often noticed that in Shakespeare, more than in other writers, critics tend to find reflections of their own views. Royalists and republicans, Tories and Whigs, colonialists and anti-colonialists, materialists and Transcendentalists, psychologists, sexual theorists, sceptics, atheists, cryptographers, Christians of most kinds and partisans of every kind – all draw support from his work. He is not more admired by men than he is by women. Occasionally one finds among admirers of Shakespeare a Calvinist or a Jewish scholar concluding that he was a Catholic; or, more commonly, a republican who deplores the way this King's Man attends to the interests of his patron; but these are exceptions to the rule. The cryptic Sonnets have often suggested to readers that Shakespeare felt and thought exactly as they do themselves. 'Shakespeare is universal!' Yes – but the mirror he holds up to nature should be used not to reflect the self but to extend and challenge the self.

A play does not have a point of view – of its nature it is neither tract nor argument nor debate, but play: a pretended re-enactment of a human situation, first complicated then finally resolved. Like other dramatists, Shakespeare imagines what participants would do, feel, think and say, and gives them words; he stands out among dramatists for his skill in this kind of ventriloquism. He lived in contentious times, and it is significant that he set only one play, *The Merry Wives of Windsor*, in the England of his own day, though its Sir John Falstaff began as a caricature of Sir John Oldcastle, a Lollard of the fifteenth century. Ben Jonson, by contrast, set several of his plays in a sharply contemporary London. Jonson often got into hot water; Shakespeare, as far as we know, did not. As already indicated, some since Keats have thought that they knew Shakespeare's point of view; earlier, he had been criticised for not having had one. 'He is so much more careful to please than to instruct, that he seems to write without any moral purpose.'[2]

'Read him therefore'

At the end of Evelyn Waugh's *A Handful of Dust* (1934), the hero is forced to read aloud to a madman in the jungle the complete works of Dickens. Once he has finished he has to start again. To reread Shakespeare would be less of a penance. Thanks to him we can better understand how we live and think. Many have thought that a good portion of human observation and wisdom is to be found in Shakespeare: John Keats wrote to Joseph Haydon in April 1817 that he was 'very near to agreeing with Hazlitt, that Shakespeare is enough for us ... He has left nothing to say about nothing or anything.'[3] Readers of Shakespeare can also share in his linguistic omnipotence. Language was to him what Ariel was to Prospero.

It is not Shakespeare's fault that he has become indispensable, that his poetic drama has become Exhibit A in the case of English Literature, or that students have to study his plays. Still less is it his fault that his writings are used and abused in support of 'Ye Olde England' tourism, or have become stepping stones in the careers of theatre directors, scholars, teachers and examinees. But Shakespeare is not easily tamed to the purposes of others. His are our best comedies, histories and tragedies: delightful, penetrating, harrowing plays rich in human life and in power of language. Quality apart, no other dramatist in English has his range. Not all literary judges admire Shakespeare, but many who are well qualified would rather have half of his plays than the rest of English Renaissance drama; some would put it much higher than that. His non-dramatic poetry is lesser, though the best of his sonnets excel other English sonnets. His 'Let the bird of loudest lay', also known as 'The Phoenix and the Turtle', is a fine mysterious poem. Many who love literature in English would not dissent from a general valuation of this kind, though they might put it differently.

For admirers of Shakespeare in the twenty-first century, however, it is sobering to think that in his lifetime his plays occupied the space which is today occupied by mass entertainment. The plays drew people from every sector of society except the poorest and the most theatre-averse, regularly filling the Globe with more people than lived in Stratford-upon-Avon. His first readers, the purchasers of the Quarto playbooks, were more literate than most theatregoers, some of whom could not read. Quarto readers also had some pocket money, but they were not, like the readers of John Donne's early verse, an intellectual coterie, nor persons of advanced taste, like the first buyers of the poetry of T. S. Eliot, Sir William Empson or Sir Geoffrey Hill. John Donne, we are told, was 'a great frequenter of plays', but some of his more serious contemporaries will have taken the view of Sir Thomas Bodley that plays were 'idle books & riffe raffes'.

Many editions of single plays by Shakespeare appeared in his lifetime. Shakespeare was not what Hamlet calls 'caviar to the general': a rarity unappreciated by the majority. Not everyone liked Shakespeare, but many people of every condition liked his work enough to pay for it regularly. It is often said, as if this were a comforting thought, that if Shakespeare were alive today he would be writing for television. This is true in one way but not in another. It is true that the Globe and the other theatres which put on the work of Kyd, Lyly, Marlowe, Shakespeare, Jonson, Chapman, Marston, Middleton, Massinger, Beaumont, Fletcher, Webster and Turner were 'popular', in the sense that everyone went to them. They were not 'popular' in another sense, that educated people avoided them. Much of the 'product' that filled Elizabethan theatres was no better than most modern film and television. Yet there is a drop in quality between Shakespeare and the best popular writing of today, and another drop between that writing and the daily fare.

In trying to account for Shakespeare's quality one should not forget his luck: an unforeseeably great opportunity opened up for him in 1594. Late Elizabethan/early Jacobean theatre was then becoming the chief outlet, and almost the only popular outlet, for a heady ferment of human issues and a swirl of ideas. This gave Shakespeare a platform on which he had useful competitors but – after the death of Marlowe and until Ben Jonson reached his peak – no major rival as a dramatist. The public stage gave an unprecedented opening to four decades of vigorous English writing. Preserved for us in the Folio, that moment outlasted Shakespeare's time by only a decade or so. It did not outlast Jonson (d.1637). English poets went on flourishing but English drama faded years before Parliament closed the theatres in 1642. Shakespeare's audiences, though varied, were unified by the shared cultural experience of a small traditional society which was undergoing radical change. That society accepted social rank in a way that ours does not, yet was not stratified and differentiated out into social classes in the way that affects the vastly greater and very urban population of today; in which, in England at least, the audience for live theatre is predominantly drawn from a narrower social range. To the extraordinary opportunity and zing of the Elizabethan theatre Shakespeare brought rare abilities, and an intelligence and ambition which made enormous demands on those abilities. He worked his talent hard, but he was lucky in his moment.

He was equally lucky in his posterity, for he wrote when the prevailing culture, medieval in its foundations, was opening up fast to the modern world. This culture, which in its educational, philosophical and moral aspects may summarily be considered as a blend of Christianity and humanism, is one that is still – with some imagination – available to us, though increasingly challenged by other ways of seeing the world. That modified continuity is one reason that Shakespeare's plays have so often been revived and can be reread without too much difficulty. Shakespeare was also lucky in that he wrote in an English which is still intelligible today – intelligible to anyone who is at home in the language, and can take the advice offered at the end of the letter in the Folio of

1623, written and signed by John Heminges and Henry Condell, but prompted in part by Ben Jonson. This letter is addressed 'To the Great Variety of Readers':

> Read him, therefore, and again, and again, and if then you do not like him, surely you are in some manifest danger not to understand him. And so we leave you to other of his friends whom if you need can be your guides: if you need them not, you can lead yourselves and others. And such readers we wish him.

Notes

Preface (pages xi–xiv)

1. Ian Donaldson (ed.), *Ben Jonson* (Oxford Authors) (Oxford: Oxford University Press, 1985). Henceforward 'Jonson'. Jonson's prefatory poem is in any Complete Shakespeare.
2. Lukas Erne, *Shakespeare as Literary Dramatist* (Cambridge: Cambridge University Press, 2003).
3. Peter Ackroyd, Introduction to the *Complete Works of Shakespeare*, ed. Peter Alexander (London: Collins, 2006).
4. 'Preface to the Edition of Shakespeare's Plays', *Samuel Johnson on Shakespeare*, ed. H. R. Woudhuysen (London: Penguin, 1989), pp. 163. Henceforward 'Johnson'.

1   First Things (pages 1–18)

1. Johnson, pp. 124–5.
2. *A New Companion to Shakespeare Studies*, ed. Kenneth Muir and Samuel Schoenbaum (Cambridge: Cambridge University Press, 1971), p. 5. Henceforward 'Camb Comp'.
3. *The Oxford Shakespeare: The Complete Sonnets and Poems*, ed. Colin Burrow (Oxford: Oxford University Press, 2002). Henceforward 'Burrow'.
4. *Diary and Letters of Madame d'Arblay* [Fanny Burney], ed. Austin Dobson, 6 vols (London: Macmillan, 1904), vol. 2, p. 344.
5. See James Shapiro, *Contested Will: Who Wrote Shakespeare?* (London: Faber and Faber, 2010).
6. Johnson, p. 136.
7. Keats completed a translation of Virgil's *Aeneid* at school, and entered Guy's Hospital by an examination which involved translating extracts from the *London Pharmacopoeia*. He thought of learning Greek, but did not do so. Thanks to Professor Nicholas Roe for these details.
8. A play looks to its theatrical future when Cassius says, after Caesar's murder, 'How many ages hence / Shall this our lofty scene be acted over, / In states unborn and accents yet unknown' (3.1.112–14). The Prologue to *Troilus and Cressida* in the Quarto looks to literature for a future, advising the 'Eternal reader' that it is 'a new play never staled with the stage, never clapper-clawed with the palms of the vulgar.'
9. See Preface, note 1.
10. Donaldson shows that we should see Jonson's hand in this epistle. Ian Donaldson, *Ben Jonson: A Life* (Oxford: Oxford University Press, 2011), p. 371. Henceforward 'Donaldson'.

11. 'Five out of six disappeared' (Donaldson, p. 123); 'conducive not prejudicial' (ibid., p. 324).
12. Alexander Pope, 'The First Epistle to the Second Book of Horace', lines 69–72.
13. Shakespeare's non-dramatic poems have all the verbal finish anyone could desire. They are not in the Folio of *Comedies, Histories and Tragedies* of 1623, nor did Pope put them in his edition of 1723. Burrow, p. 8.
14. Pope could have known Jonson's reported view that 'Shakespeare wanted art' from Drummond's *Conversations*, part published in 1711. See Jonson, p. 596 and endnotes.
15. Johnson, p. 147.

2   The Recorded Life (pages 19–27)

1. *Palladis Tamia*, in vol. 2 of G. Gregory Smith (ed.), *Elizabethan Critical Essays* (Oxford: Oxford University Press, 1904).
2. Jonson, p. 539. Shakespeare was later reported by the son of a fellow player to have been 'very good company and of a very ready and pleasant smooth wit', but not 'a company keeper'. If so, he was unlike the noisy Christopher Marlowe and Ben Jonson. If his acting was similarly discreet, he was more of an Alec Guinness than a Laurence Olivier. See Katherine Duncan-Jones, *Ungentle Shakespeare* (London: Arden Shakespeare, 2001).
3. See Germaine Greer, *Shakespeare's Wife* (London: Bloomsbury, 2007).
4. For the stiff classical regime at Westminster School, see Donaldson, pp. 69–82.
5. *Brief Lives by John Aubrey, A Selection*, ed. Richard Barber (London: The Folio Society, 1975), p. 280.
6. Emrys Jones, *The Origins of Shakespeare* (Oxford: Oxford University Press, 1977), p. 263. Henceforward 'Jones'.
7. *Palladis Tamia*, Camb Comp, p. 58.
8. Susanna and Judith are heroines of books regarded as canonical in Catholic bibles but as deuterocanonical in Protestant bibles.

3   Plays (pages 28–31)

1. See under Bodley in *The Oxford Companion to Shakespeare*, ed. Michael Dobson and Stanley Wells (Oxford: Oxford University Press, 2001). Henceforward 'Ox Comp'.
2. Johnson, p. 132. The 'Unities': neoclassical theorists held that the action of a play should tell a single story of events enacted in one place at one time, either on a single day, or in three hours.
3. Playing: Helen Cooper, Professor of Medieval and Renaissance English at Cambridge, usefully summarises the legacy of medieval

drama in *Shakespeare and the Medieval World*, Arden Companions to Shakespeare (London: A. & C. Black, 2010).

4. Johnson., p. 125.

4   Shake-scene (pages 32–48)

1. Edmund Malone, *An Historical Account of the English Stage*, 1790; from Jonathan Bate (ed.), *The Romantics on Shakespeare* (London: Penguin, 1997), p. 56. Henceforward 'Bate'.
2. See Brian Vickers, *Shakespeare, Co-Author: A Historical Study of Five Collaborative Plays* (Oxford: Oxford University Press, 2004).
3. This is examined at several points in Jones, *The Origins of Shakespeare*. See Chapter 11, note 4.
4. Camb Comp, p. 77.
5. Fully traced out in Sir Frank Kermode, *Shakespeare's Language* (London: Allen Lane, 2000). Henceforward 'Kermode'.

6   Histories (pages 62–72)

1. 'Shakespeare's poems [*sic*] are a great animated fair; and it is to his own country that he owes his riches.' His Romans 'are Englishmen to the bone; but they are human, thoroughly human, and thus the Roman toga ... fits them.' J. W. von Goethe, *Wilhelm Meister's Apprenticeship*, 1795–6, trans. T. Carlyle (1823). Bate, p. 70.
2. See Stephen Greenblatt, *Will in the World: How Shakespeare Became Shakespeare* (New York: W. W. Norton, 2004).

7   *The Merchant of Venice* and the Whirligig of Time (pages 73–85)

1. The 1598 entry in the Stationers' Register – 'a book of the Marchaunt of Venyce, or otherwise called the Jewe of Venyce' – suggests that the play had from the beginning a dual focus.
2. On usury, see *The Merchant of Venice*, ed. M. Merchant, New Penguin Shakespeare (Harmondsworth: Penguin, 1967), p. 173. Canon law distinguished between loans productive of the public good and non-productive loans.
3. Three Gospels tell how at Gadara in Galilee, Jesus of Nazareth frees a demoniac of the evil spirits which possess him. Jesus sends them into a herd of pigs, which runs over a cliff (Matthew 5, Mark 8, Luke 8).
4. 'Cut-throat' may allude to legends such as that told by Chaucer's Prioress.
5. A point I owe to Professor Neil Rhodes.
6. The form used in the Bishops' Bible, the version prescribed to be read aloud in church.

7. *The English Auden*, ed. E. Mendelson (London: Faber and Faber, 1977), p. 242; the line quoted in the following paragraph is from Yeats's 'The Circus Animals' Desertion'.

8   To the Globe (pages 86–99)

1. 'In his comic scenes he is seldom very successful, when he engages his characters in reciprocations of smartness and contests of sarcasm; their jests are commonly gross and their pleasantry licentious.' Johnson, p. 131.
2. James Shapiro, *1599: A Year in the Life of William Shakespeare* (London: Faber and Faber, 2005).
3. 'Neither his gentlemen nor his ladies have much delicacy, nor are sufficiently distinguished from his clowns by any appearance of refined manners.' Johnson, p. 131.
4. 'The woman shall not wear that which pertaineth unto a man, neither shall a man put on a woman's garment: for all that do so are abomination unto the Lord thy God' (Deuteronomy 20:5).
5. See Donaldson, p. 107.

9   Horatio's Question (pages 100–109)

1. The literal translation of Max Hayward and Manya Harari in the first English edition of 1958. The poem was recited at Pasternak's funeral. *Dr Zhivago* (London: Collins, 1958).
2. Johnson, p. 163.
3. William Shakespeare, *Hamlet*, ed. Harold Jenkins (London: Methuen, 1982), p. 83.

11   Tragedies (pages 120–139)

1. *Hamlet*, ed. Jenkins, p. 407.
2. Thomas Rymer, in his *Short View of Tragedy* (1693), thought *Othello* 'a caution to all Maidens of Quality how, without their Parents consent, they run away with Blackamoors'. See Honigmann's Arden edition of *Othello*, pp. 3, 14–31.
3. One example is Prince Hal, at *1 Henry IV*, 1.2.199.
4. Quarto reads 'Indian', Folio 'Iudean'. Honigmann, pp. 342–3, discusses the merits of each reading. Kermode, pp. 181–2, prefers *Iudean*. Emrys Jones in *The Origins of Shakespeare* shows how Shakespeare's early plays used the central event of medieval drama, the Passion, to deepen tragic pathos, giving secular tragedy a borrowed Christian weight, which by 1630 it had lost. See Chapter 4, note 3.

5. For Johnson's protest, see Johnson, p. 222. Tate's version is available on the Internet (http://archive.org/stream/historyofkinglea00shak#page/14/mode/2up), along with the reasons he gave for the changes he made: 'I found the whole ... a Heap of Jewels, unstrung and unpolisht; yet so dazling in their Disorder, that I soon perceiv'd I had seiz'd a Treasure. 'Twas my good Fortune to light on one Expedient to rectifie what was wanting in the Regularity and Probability of the Tale, which was to run through the whole a Love betwixt Edgar and Cordelia, that never chang'd word with each other in the Original. This renders Cordelia's Indifference and her Father's Passion in the first Scene probable ...' Tate's play ends thus:

> *Edgar*:   Our drooping Country now erects her Head,
> Peace spreads her balmy Wings, and Plenty Blooms.
> Divine Cordelia, all the Gods can witness
> How much thy Love to Empire I prefer!
> Thy bright Example shall convince the World
> (Whatever Storms of Fortune are decreed)
> That Truth and Vertue shall at last succeed.

6. Peter Brook's 1962 production, made into a memorable film, cut some positive moments.
7. See Foakes's note to 5.3.304, Lear's last moment, in *King Lear*, ed. R. A. Foakes (London: Arden Shakespeare, 1997), p. 390.
8. Johnson, p. 220.
9. Clare Asquith, *Shadowplay* (New York: Perseus, 2005), p. 221.
10. In *The Winter's Tale* Cleomenes describes the temple of Apollo in similar terms: 'The climate's delicate, the air most sweet, / Fertile the isle, the temple much surpassing / The common praise it bears' (3.1.1–3).

12   Late Romances (pages 140–155)

1. The Oxford editors of *Cymbeline* show that the Folio's Imogen may be a misprint for Innogen. The name Cordelia is found in Shakespeare's sources in various forms; he chose a form close to the Greek and Latin words for 'heart'.
2. But see 'Why, all the souls that were, were forfeit once, / And He that might have the vantage best have took / Found out the remedy' – *Measure for Measure* (2.2.73–5). Shakespeare's poem 'The Phoenix and the Turtle' assumes familiarity with scholastic theology. See Burrow, p. 374.
3. 'Empire' was first used of England in the Act of Supremacy of 1534, drafted by Thomas Cromwell for Henry VIII. The Act claimed that a self-governing England had never acknowledged Roman jurisdiction even in matters spiritual. 'Empire' meant self-rule, not rule over others.
4. Kermode, p. 291. Kermode's Preface (p. viii) mentions attitudes to Shakespeare he particularly disliked: 'the worst of them maintains

that the reputation of Shakespeare is fraudulent, the result of an eighteenth-century nationalist or imperialist plot. A related notion, almost equally presumptuous, is that to make sense of Shakespeare we need first to see the plays as involved in the political discourse of his day to a degree that has only now become intelligible.'

13 Retrospect (pages 156–161)

1. Johnson, p. 139.
2. Ibid., p. 130.
3. Bate, p. 197.

Further Reading

Editions of Shakespeare

A Complete Works is indispensible. Recommended are those of Peter Alexander (1951, 2006) and the Compact Oxford edition, edited by Stanley Wells and Gary Taylor (1988); the latter has a headnote to each play; both have introductions but no other notes. Four annotated complete editions can be recommended: (1) *The Norton Shakespeare*, edited by Stephen Greenblatt et al. (1997), a version of the Oxford text; (2) *The Riverside Shakespeare* (2nd edn), edited by Gwynne Blakemore Evans et al. (1997); (3) *The Arden Shakespeare Complete Works*, edited by Richard Proudfoot, Ann Thompson and David Scott Kastan (1988); (4) the Royal Shakespeare Company edition, edited by Jonathan Bate and Eric Rasmussen (2007).

Texts vary with editorial policy. Alexander, Arden and Riverside are composite texts, but the Oxford breaks with this tradition, and Bate/Rasmussen gives primacy to the Folio text. The Oxford Shakespeare, which did away with the accepted tradition of the composite or 'conflated' text, has had much success, so that the texts of a few plays, notably *Hamlet* and *King Lear*, differ greatly from edition to edition.

The one-volume Completes outsell the multi-volume versions, but an annotated Complete is unwieldy, a book for a desk. The only handy one-volume Complete is the unannotated Peter Alexander. Completes have different running orders: some group by genre, like the Folio, and follow its order; others follow chronological order within a genre group; most now ignore genre and go for chronology.

Single plays

Editions of individual plays are far more pleasant to use, and readers can choose one with as much introduction, annotation and glossary as required. Good old series include those in Signet or Penguin. The scholarly Arden series is now into its third cycle. Other scholarly series in progress are the Oxford and the New Cambridge editions, as is also the RSC. Oxford, Arden and New Cambridge are good, but the best or most suitable editions are not all in one series. The most recent edition is not always best. One solution is to buy an unannotated Complete but single plays in annotated editions.

Quotations and line references

Different readers have different editions, and their line references may differ. In *Reading Shakespeare*, quotations and references are deliberately taken from a variety of editions. The lineation of verse, sometimes set as prose in early printings, is now settled – unless the act and scene divisions, or the texts themselves, differ. The lineation of prose varies with the width of the text column and the size of the type.

Complete Works

Complete Works of Shakespeare. Ed. P. Alexander. London: Collins, 2006.

William Shakespeare: The Complete Works. Compact Edition. Ed. S. Wells and G. Taylor. Oxford: Oxford University Press, 1988.

The Norton Shakespeare. Ed. S. Greenblatt et al. London: W. W. Norton, 1997.

The Riverside Shakespeare. 2nd edn. Ed. G. Blakemore Evans et al. Boston: Houghton Mifflin, 1997.

The Arden Shakespeare Complete Works. Ed. R. Proudfoot, A. Thompson and D. Scott Kastan. London: Arden, 1988.

The RSC Shakespeare Complete Works. Ed. J. Bate and E. Rasmussen. Basingstoke: Palgrave Macmillan, 2007.

Single editions referred to in this book

Hamlet (Arden Shakespeare). Ed. H. Jenkins. London: Methuen, 1982.

King Lear (Arden Shakespeare). Ed. R. A. Foakes. London: Methuen, 1997.

Love's Labour's Lost (Oxford Shakespeare). Ed. G. R. Hibbard. Oxford: Oxford University Press, 1990.

Macbeth (New Cambridge Shakespeare). Ed. A. R. Braunmuller. Cambridge: Cambridge University Press, 1997.

Othello (Arden Shakespeare). Ed. E. A. J. Honigmann. London: Methuen, 1997.

The Complete Sonnets and Poems (Oxford Shakespeare). Ed. C. Burrow. Oxford: Oxford University Press, 2002.

Commentary

Bate, J., ed. *The Romantics on Shakespeare*. London: Penguin, 1997. A useful anthology.

Bradley, A. C. *Shakespearean Tragedy*. London: Macmillan, 1904. Still going strong.

Cooper, H. *Shakespeare and the Medieval World* (Arden Companions to Shakespeare). London: A. & C. Black, 2010. A compact reminder of what is too often forgotten.

Dobson, M. and S. Wells, eds. *Oxford Companion to Shakespeare*. Oxford: Oxford University Press, 2001. De luxe, and almost comprehensive.

Donaldson, I., ed. *Ben Jonson* (Oxford Authors). Oxford: Oxford University Press, 1985. The standard edition.

Donaldson, I. *Ben Jonson. A Life*. Oxford: Oxford University Press, 2011. Detailed account of a life better documented than Shakespeare's.

Duncan-Jones, K. *Ungentle Shakespeare: Scenes from His Life*. London: Arden Shakespeare, 2001. Puts the working life in context. Stimulating.

Erne, L. *Shakespeare as Literary Dramatist*. Cambridge: Cambridge University Press, 2003. Persuasively argues its case from the bibliographical record.

Greenblatt, S. *Will in the World: How Shakespeare Became Shakespeare*. New York: W. W. Norton, 2004. A different contextualisation.

Johnson, S. 'Preface to the Edition of Shakespeare's Plays'. In *Samuel Johnson on Shakespeare*. Ed. H. R.Woudhuysen. London: Penguin, 1989. The best pre-academic account.

Jones, E. *The Origins of Shakespeare*. Oxford: Oxford University Press, 1977. Still a pioneer study.

Kermode, F. *Shakespeare's Language*. London: Allen Lane, 2000. Close analysis by an expert critic.

Muir, K. and S. Schoenbaum, eds. *A New Companion to Shakespeare Studies*. Cambridge: Cambridge University Press, 1971. Still handy.

Palfrey, S. and T. Stern. *Shakespeare in Parts*. Oxford: Oxford University Press, 2007. New stuff on the acting.

Shapiro, J. *Contested Will: Who Wrote Shakespeare?* London: Faber and Faber, 2010. The authorship controversy put to bed.

Smith, E. *The Cambridge Introduction to Shakespeare*. Cambridge: Cambridge University Press, 2007. A well-edited selection of commissioned essays.

Vickers, B. *Shakespeare, Co-Author: A Historical Study of Five Collaborative Plays*. Oxford: Oxford University Press, 2004. New light.

Index

Page numbers in *italics* denote an illustration